SLICES OF (MOBILE) LIFE
A SOCIOLOGICAL STUDY AND MANIFESTO ON WORK-RELATED HIGH MOBILITY

Directors of publication:
Christophe Gay, Sylvie Landriève and Marc Pearce / Mobile Lives Forum

Publisher:
Anne Zweibaum with Emmanuel Daemers

Book Design:
Christian Kirk-Jensen / Danish Pastry Design

Conception of the visualization of the data:
Marc Pearce

Colorization of drawings:
Léa Mazé

Translation from french to english:
Jessica Strelec

Proofreading:
Rick Willett and Jessica Strelec

Photoengraving:
Zincograf

ISBN : 978-2-9195073-13
Legal deposit: october 2014
Printed in Italy

© Éditions Loco-L'Atelier d'édition / Mobile Lives Forum, 2014

SLICES OF (MOBILE) LIFE

A SOCIOLOGICAL STUDY AND MANIFESTO ON WORK-RELATED HIGH MOBILITY

EMMANUEL RAVALET,
STÉPHANIE VINCENT-GESLIN,
VINCENT KAUFMANN
ADAPTATION AND DRAWINGS BY **JEAN LEVEUGLE**

SIX PORTRAITS OF MOBILE LIFE
JEAN, EMILIE, MARTIN, GABY, THIERRY AND CHRISTELLE ARE JUST LIKE A LOT OF US—'HIGHLY MOBILE', THAT IS..........................P 7

BEHIND THE DRAWINGS
UNDERSTANDING 'HIGHLY MOBILE' LIFESTYLES, AND THE TRADE-OFFS BETWEEN PERSONAL LIFE, WORKING LIFE, AND TRAVEL......................P 45

POLITICAL DESIGNS
OUR RECOMMENDATIONS FOR ACKNOWLEDGING THE ASPIRATIONS OF 'HIGHLY MOBILE PEOPLE' AND MAKING THEIR LIVES EASIER...................P 69

SIX PORTRAITS OF MOBILE LIFE

JEAN

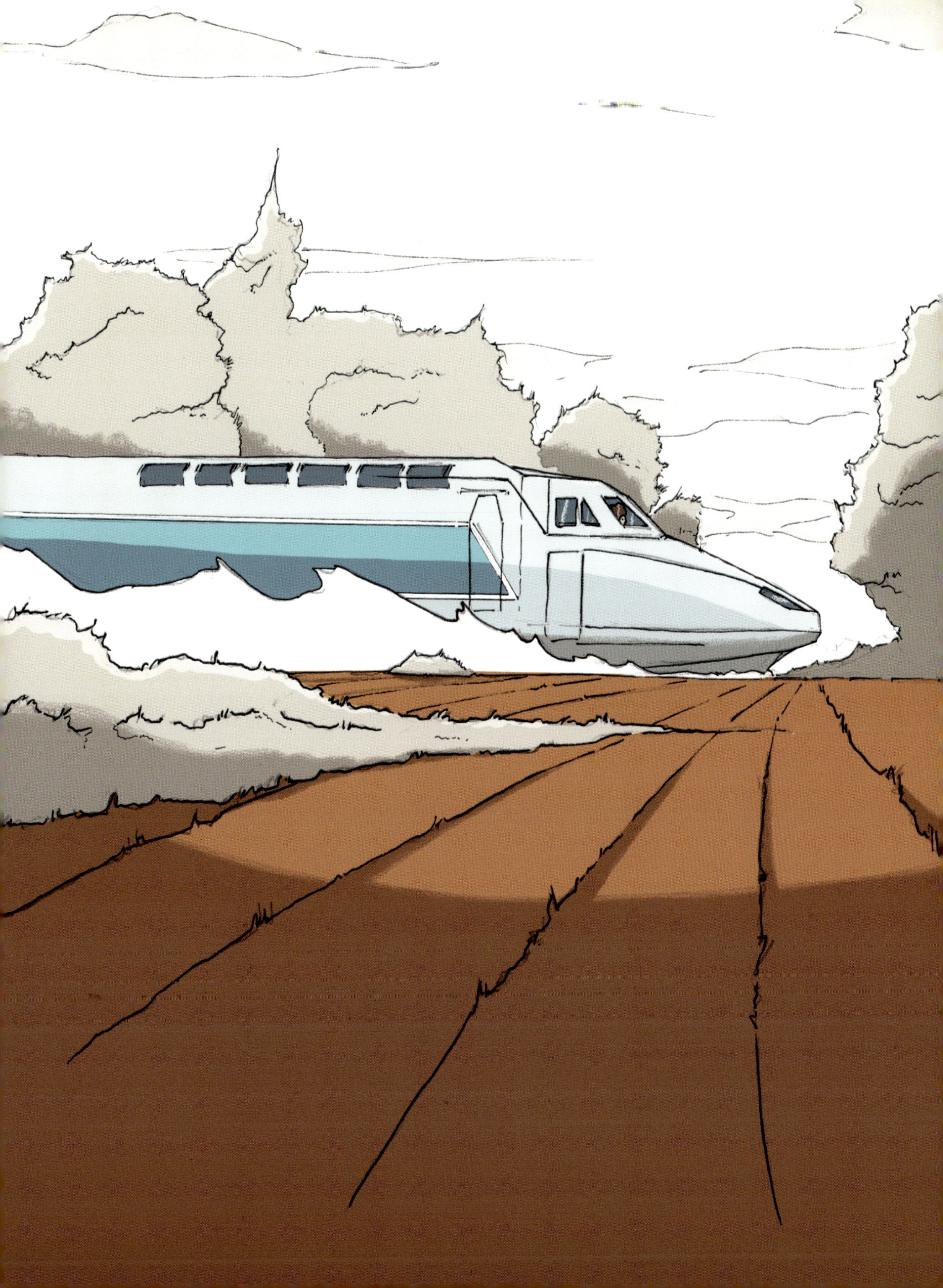

8:04 AM. SNCF DORMITORY IN QUIMPER
TOU ES ROMANTICAAAA... ROMANTIQUE ET BOHÉMMMME.. TU T'EN DÉFENDS PARFOIS, MAIS MOI JE SAIS, JE SAIS TOUT ÇAAAA...CLIC!
YOU SEE, JEAN-LUC, IT'S THE ECONOMIC CRISIS. THAT'S SLOWING DOWN GROWTH, TOO.
YEAH, BUT THE CRISIS HAS BEEN GOING ON FOR YEARS NOW!
WE CAN'T LIVE LIKE OUR PARENTS DID, PHILIPPE. WE'RE GOING TO HAVE TO TIGHTEN OUR BELTS.
MHHH...
AND THAT MEANS ADJUSTING OUR BUDGETS.
ALL RIGHT, BUT JUST LET ME ADJUST MY SHIRT FIRST.
MORNING, AMIN. SLEEP WELL?
NOT TOO BAD, THANKS. GOING HOME TO THE WIFE AND KIDS TONIGHT?
YEAH, WE'RE HAVING DINNER TOGETHER.
WHAT ABOUT YOU?
NO, TOMORROW.
TONIGHT TOULOUSE.

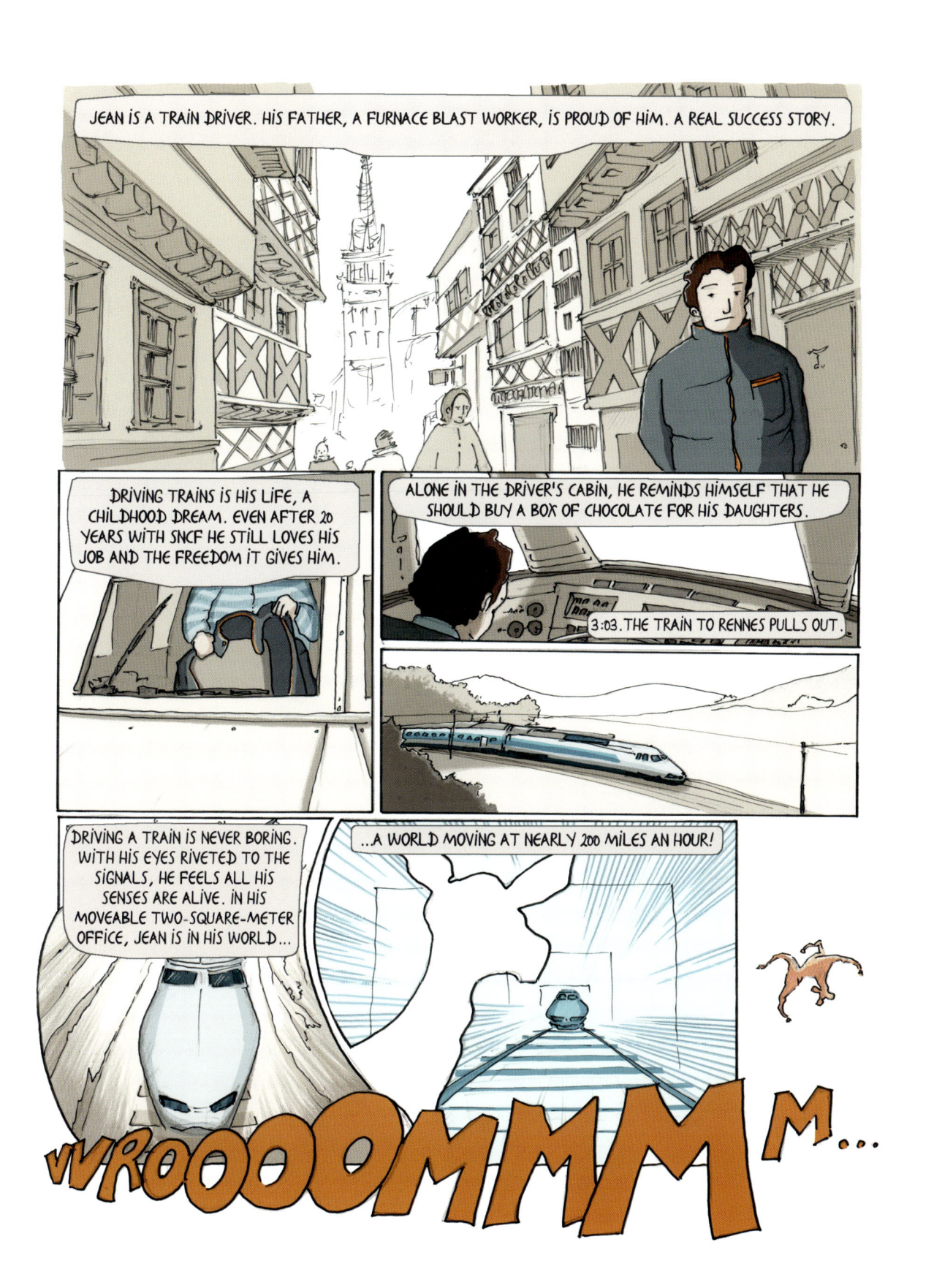

JEAN IS A TRAIN DRIVER. HIS FATHER, A FURNACE BLAST WORKER, IS PROUD OF HIM. A REAL SUCCESS STORY.

DRIVING TRAINS IS HIS LIFE, A CHILDHOOD DREAM. EVEN AFTER 20 YEARS WITH SNCF HE STILL LOVES HIS JOB AND THE FREEDOM IT GIVES HIM.

ALONE IN THE DRIVER'S CABIN, HE REMINDS HIMSELF THAT HE SHOULD BUY A BOX OF CHOCOLATE FOR HIS DAUGHTERS.

3:03. THE TRAIN TO RENNES PULLS OUT.

DRIVING A TRAIN IS NEVER BORING. WITH HIS EYES RIVETED TO THE SIGNALS, HE FEELS ALL HIS SENSES ARE ALIVE. IN HIS MOVEABLE TWO-SQUARE-METER OFFICE, JEAN IS IN HIS WORLD...

...A WORLD MOVING AT NEARLY 200 MILES AN HOUR!

VVROOOOMMMM...

HEY !
CLICK.
TRAFFIC CONTROL? 8046 DRIVER HERE. I'VE JUST MADE AN EMERGENCY STOP.
OK. HOW LONG WILL YOU BE THERE ?
I'LL CHECK AND GET BACK TO YOU.
CLICK.
DAMMIT! WITH THIS ANIMAL ON THE TRACKS...
...I'LL NEVER GET HOME ON TIME!
6:11PM. THE TRAIN ARRIVES AT PARIS-MONTPARNASSE STATION 50 MINUTES LATE. THE REST OF THE TRIP WENT SMOOTHLY, BUT NOT AT FULL SPEED.
JEAN STILL HAS TO FILL OUT THE ACCIDENT REPORT BEFORE CATCHING THE TRAIN TO LE MANS. THIS TIME, HOWEVER, HE'S A PASSENGER.
DURING THE TRIP HE CHATS WITH A COUPLE OF CO-WORKERS.
7:48 PM. JEAN ARRIVES IN LE MANS. WITH THE ACCIDENT AND ALL, HE FORGOT TO GET CHOCOLATES IN PARIS. FINDING SOMETHING OPEN AT THIS HOUR IN LE MANS WILL BE HARD. HE WALKS TO HIS CAR WITH A SLIGHT SENSE OF FOREBODING.

AT DINNER, JEAN TRIES TO FOLLOW HIS WIFE AND DAUGHTERS' DISCUSSION. HE FEELS OUT OF PLACE, ALOOF.

IT'S HARD FOR HIM TO JOIN IN THE CONVERSATION.

ELSA HAS PROBLEMS WITH HER ENGLISH TEACHER?

LILOU HAS A BOYFRIEND?

AND NICOLE... NICOLE?

THIS EVENING, AND MORE AND MORE OFTEN, THE CONNECTION JUST ISN'T THERE. THE INSINUATIONS, THE INNUENDOS, THE THINLY-VEILED REPROACHES.

JEAN TRIES TO EXPLAIN. THE ACCIDENT, HIS LATE ARRIVAL, THE CHOCOLATES HE'D HOPED TO BRING... IN VAIN.

TOMORROW NICOLE IS GETTING UP EARLY TO GO TO THE GYM WITH BRIGITTE AND LAURENCE. FOR ONCE, JEAN WILL BE THE ONE DRIVING THE GIRLS TO SCHOOL. FEELING A BIT LOST, HE GOES UP TO BED. SOMETIMES, HE WONDERS JUST WHERE "HOME" REALLY IS.

EMILIE

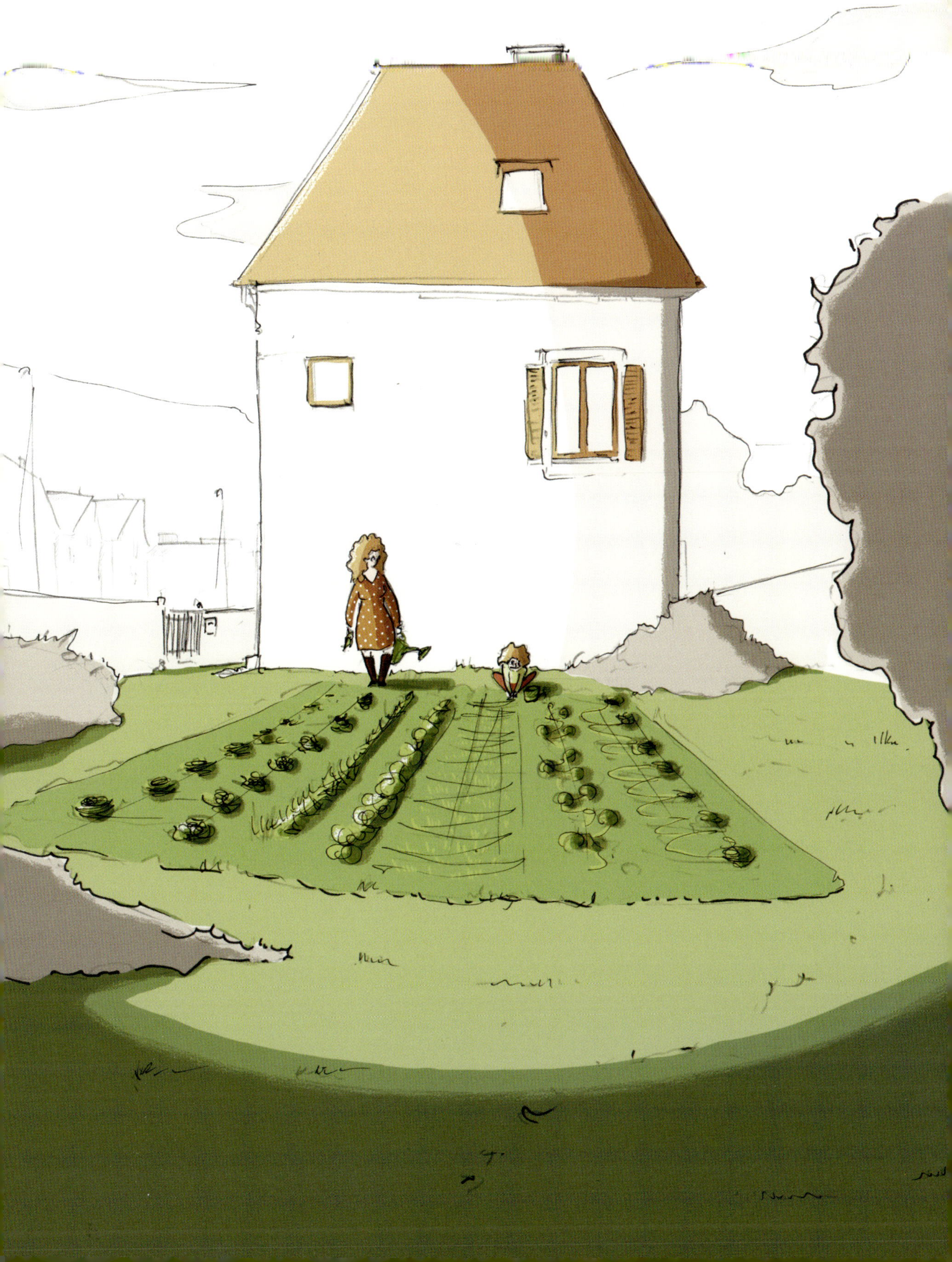

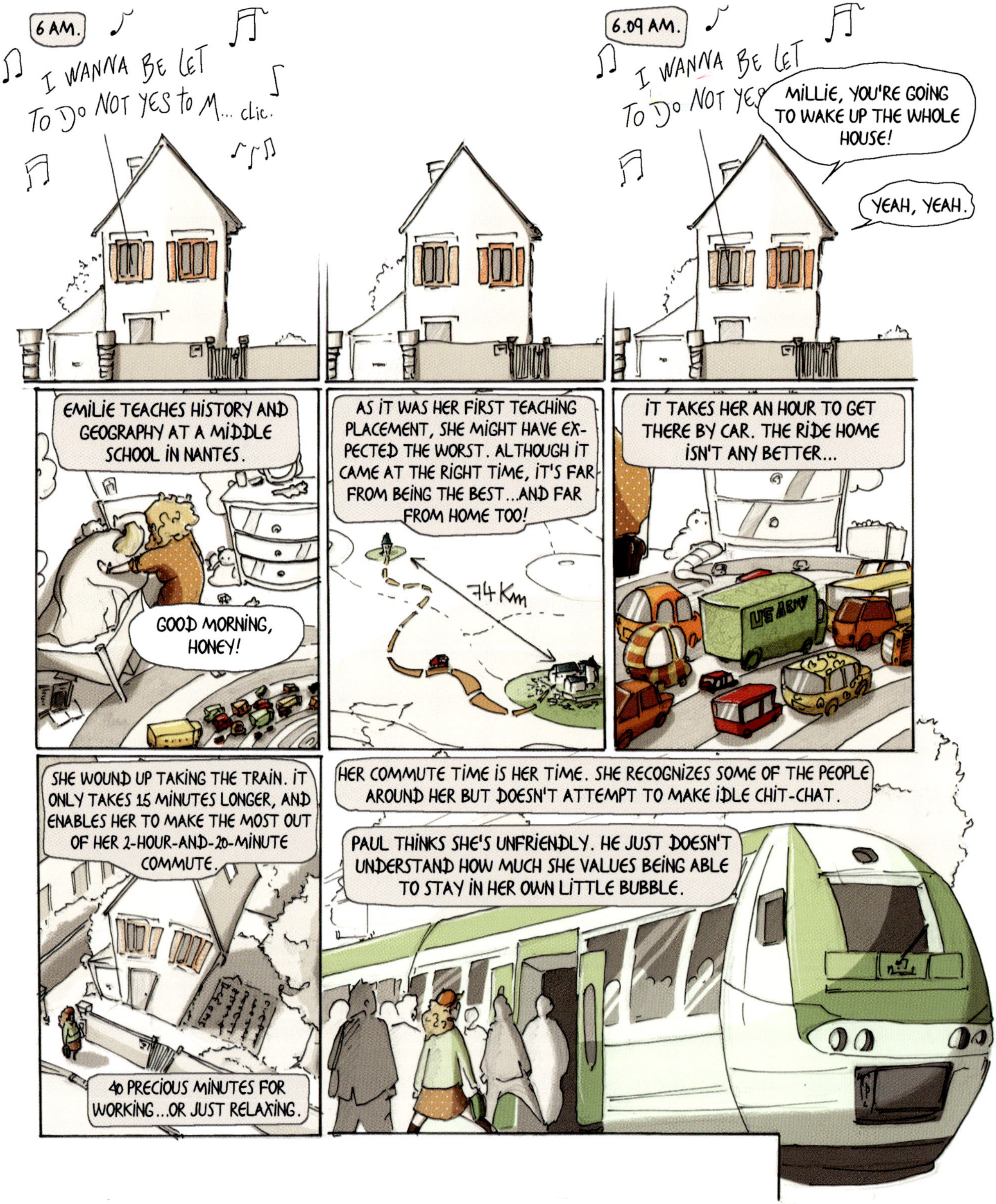
6 AM.
I WANNA BE LET TO DO NOT YES TO M... CLIC.
EMILIE TEACHES HISTORY AND GEOGRAPHY AT A MIDDLE SCHOOL IN NANTES.
GOOD MORNING, HONEY!
AS IT WAS HER FIRST TEACHING PLACEMENT, SHE MIGHT HAVE EXPECTED THE WORST. ALTHOUGH IT CAME AT THE RIGHT TIME, IT'S FAR FROM BEING THE BEST...AND FAR FROM HOME TOO!
74 Km
6.09 AM.
I WANNA BE LET TO DO NOT YES
MILLIE, YOU'RE GOING TO WAKE UP THE WHOLE HOUSE!
YEAH, YEAH.
IT TAKES HER AN HOUR TO GET THERE BY CAR. THE RIDE HOME ISN'T ANY BETTER...
SHE WOUND UP TAKING THE TRAIN. IT ONLY TAKES 15 MINUTES LONGER, AND ENABLES HER TO MAKE THE MOST OUT OF HER 2-HOUR-AND-20-MINUTE COMMUTE.
40 PRECIOUS MINUTES FOR WORKING...OR JUST RELAXING.
HER COMMUTE TIME IS HER TIME. SHE RECOGNIZES SOME OF THE PEOPLE AROUND HER BUT DOESN'T ATTEMPT TO MAKE IDLE CHIT-CHAT.
PAUL THINKS SHE'S UNFRIENDLY. HE JUST DOESN'T UNDERSTAND HOW MUCH SHE VALUES BEING ABLE TO STAY IN HER OWN LITTLE BUBBLE.

Teaching middle school requires a lot of work outside the classroom. Emilie can usually get some of it taken care of on the regional express train. But she always sets aside a bit of time to work on her history programme for the local radio station.

She settles into her cocoon - a seat with no one facing her, obviously - with her papers, books, cookies and thermos of coffee. Time seems to fly when she's on the train, like when she's sleeping.

Her teaching diploma in hand, she got a job, started a family and started thinking about her future.

Teaching is a real vocation. Emilie enjoys watching her students' progress. To pique their curiosity, she shares her passion for local Anjou heritage, especially the Middle Ages.

WOW, PEOPLE STILL DRIVE THOSE THINGS?
HE MUST SPEND LOADS OF TIME POLISHING THAT ONE.
NO ONE CAN SAY WE DON'T KNOW HOW TO TAKE CARE OF OUR ANCIENT HERITAGE HERE, IN ANJOU...
EMILIE IS ALWAYS HAPPY WHEN SHE GETS TO SCHOOL. FOR NOW, SHE ACCEPTS THE LONG COMMUTE. BUT SOMETIMES IT WEIGHS ON HER. IT'S HARD TO GET INVOLVED OUTSIDE OF THE CLASSROOM.
BY THE WAY, DID YOU ASK FOR YOUR TRANSFER ?
YEAH, BUT IT'LL TAKE A GOOD FIVE YEARS.
I DON'T KNOW HOW YOU DO IT. I MOVED CLOSER TO THE SCHOOL AFTER SIX MONTHS.
THAT REMINDS ME, TARIK GOT A POSITION IN NANTES. HE'S CELEBRATING TONIGHT. I IMAGINE YOU CAN'T MAKE IT THOUGH...
WELL, IT'S A BIT COMPLICATED. AND, YOU KNOW, I HARDLY KNOW TARIK. WE RARELY RUN INTO EACH OTHER.
OBVIOUSLY, IF I NEVER GO TO CLASS COUNCIL OR MEETINGS, I'LL NEVER GET TO KNOW MY COLLEAGUES. BUT THE LAST TRAIN IS AT 6:39 PM....
MOVE OR WAIT FOR A TRANSFER? THE FIRST IS OUT OF THE QUESTION. PAUL AND EMILIE HAVE JUST BOUGHT A HOUSE TOGETHER. THEY'VE BEEN DOING RENOVATIONS AND AREN'T READY TO SIMPLY UP AND LEAVE.

AND THEY'VE MANAGED TO GET A SPOT IN DAY CARE FOR LILA, WHICH WOULD BE CRAZY TO GIVE UP. NOT TO MENTION THE ADDED BENEFIT OF HAVING:

HER PARENTS,
HER IN-LAWS,
AND HER FRIENDS, } ALL WITHIN EASY REACH.

PAUL WOULDN'T DREAM OF LETTING GO OF HIS PERMANENT CONTRACT EITHER, ESPECIALLY NOWADAYS.

THERE'S NO SHORT-TERM SOLUTION: EMILIE WILL CONTINUE COMMUTING FOR THE NEXT SEVERAL YEARS.

OH...

NO WAY! HE SPENT THE DAY WATCHING TRAINS GO BY?

THAT GUY'S GOT IT EASY.

6:26 PM. EMILIE GETS OFF THE TRAIN AND HURRIES HOME TO FIND HER FAMILY WAITING FOR HER.

10:15 PM. EXHAUSTED, SHE GOES TO BED BEFORE PAUL. THE PAST FEW NIGHTS, SHE'S GONE TO BED BEFORE HIM. SHE SPENDS ALMOST 2½ HOURS A DAY COMMUTING. IT'S THE LESSER EVIL: ONLY A FEW MORE YEARS.

MARTIN

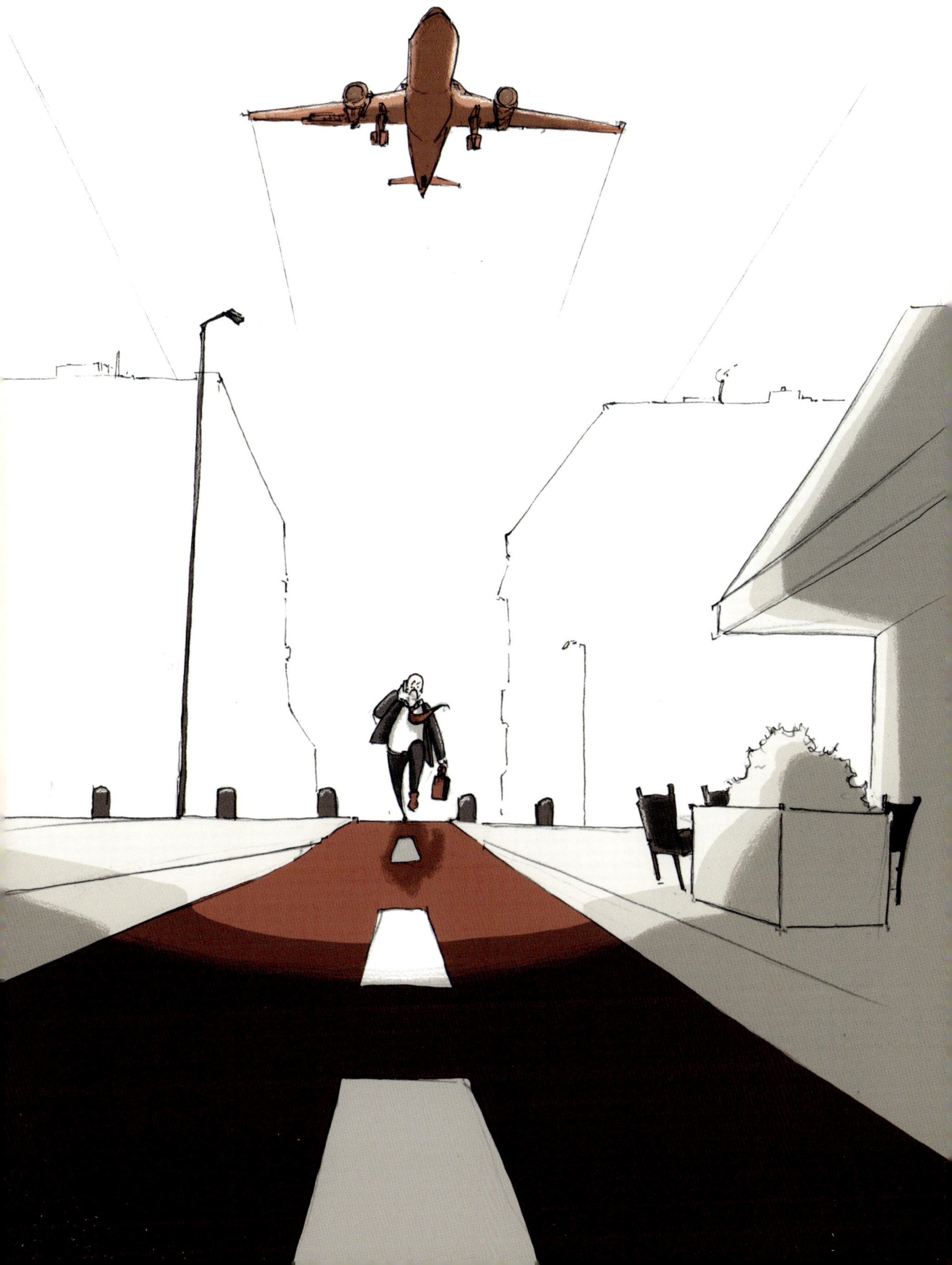

6:09 AM. MARTIN IS ALREADY AWAKE. HE TURNS OFF HIS ALARM BEFORE IT EVEN HAS A CHANCE TO GO OFF AND HEADS FOR THE BATHROOM.

MARTIN HAS BEEN A SALES REP FOR 26 YEARS.

IN SHOES FOR 17.

HIS FINE BOOTS...

...CARRY HIM SEVEN LEAGUES IN A SINGLE BOUND.

OR ALMOST.

7:00 AM. BECAUSE IT'S STILL EARLY, MARTIN DOESN'T SAY GOODBYE TO LÉA OR THEIR FOUR CHILDREN. HE MUSTN'T BE LATE. HE'S GOT A BUSY DAY AHEAD OF HIM: NANTES, RENNES, THEN MARSEILLE VIA PARIS.

MARTIN, A BIG TRAVELLER SINCE CHILDHOOD, HAS A THIRST FOR DISCOVERY AND ADVENTURE. HE'S AS COMFORTABLE DRIVING AS IN THE MÉTRO, TRAIN STATIONS OR AIRPORTS.

THE MANY PLACES HE'S BEEN TO HAVE MADE HIM A REAL GEOGRAPHY WIZ, NOT TO MENTION A GENIUS WHEN IT COMES TO MANAGING HIS TIME.

MARTIN KNOWS HOW TO ADAPT TO THE DIFFERENT PEOPLE HE MEETS - BE IT RICH MANUFACTURERS, MEGASTORE EMPLOYEES, OR A FOREMAN FROM THE VALLÉE DE ROMANS OR THE GUANGDONG PROVINCE.

AN EXCEPTIONAL PRODUCT...

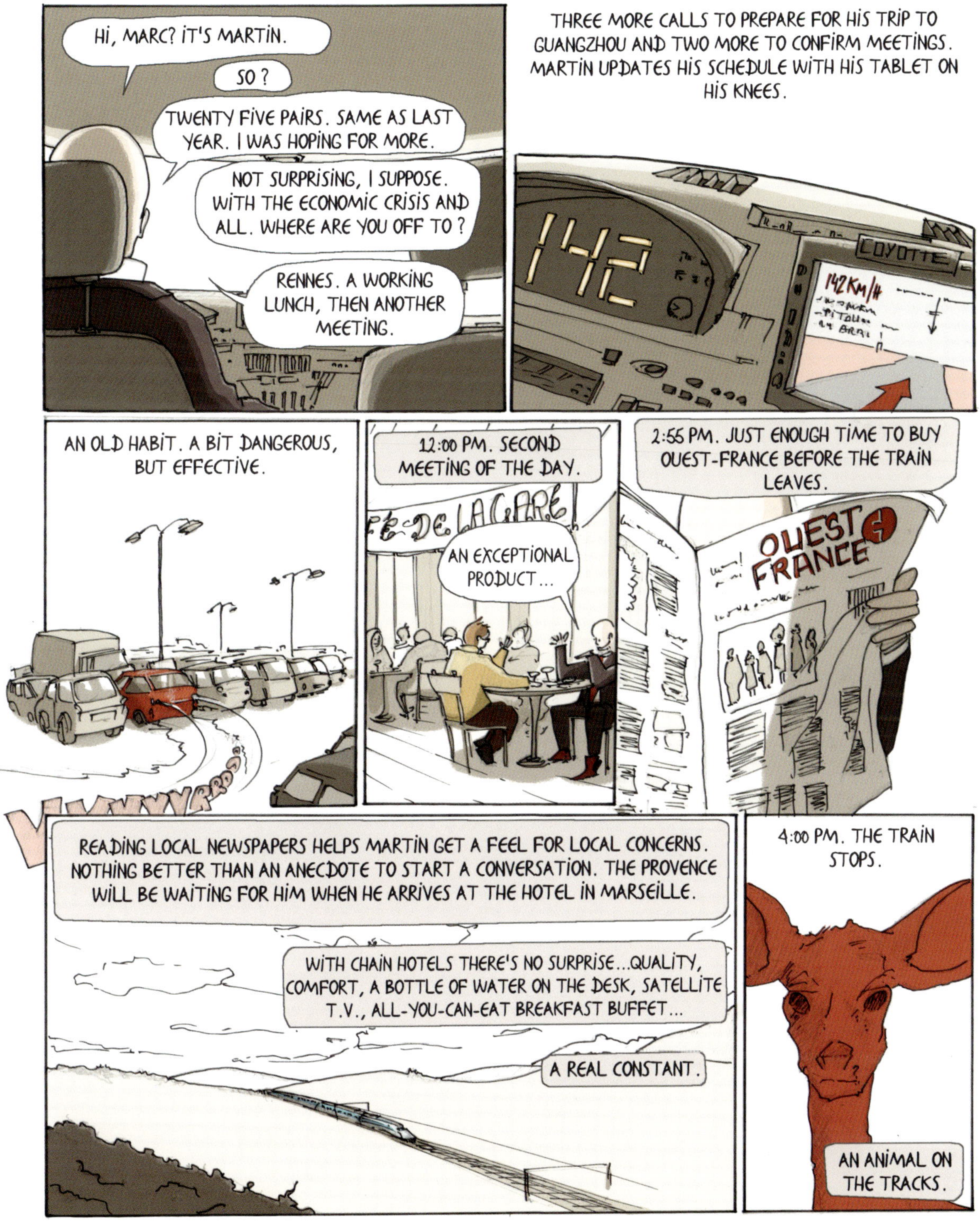

HI, MARC? IT'S MARTIN.
SO?
TWENTY FIVE PAIRS. SAME AS LAST YEAR. I WAS HOPING FOR MORE.
NOT SURPRISING, I SUPPOSE. WITH THE ECONOMIC CRISIS AND ALL. WHERE ARE YOU OFF TO?
RENNES. A WORKING LUNCH, THEN ANOTHER MEETING.
THREE MORE CALLS TO PREPARE FOR HIS TRIP TO GUANGZHOU AND TWO MORE TO CONFIRM MEETINGS. MARTIN UPDATES HIS SCHEDULE WITH HIS TABLET ON HIS KNEES.
142
COYOTTE
142 KM/H
AN OLD HABIT. A BIT DANGEROUS, BUT EFFECTIVE.
12:00 PM. SECOND MEETING OF THE DAY.
AN EXCEPTIONAL PRODUCT...
2:55 PM. JUST ENOUGH TIME TO BUY OUEST-FRANCE BEFORE THE TRAIN LEAVES.
OUEST FRANCE
READING LOCAL NEWSPAPERS HELPS MARTIN GET A FEEL FOR LOCAL CONCERNS. NOTHING BETTER THAN AN ANECDOTE TO START A CONVERSATION. THE PROVENCE WILL BE WAITING FOR HIM WHEN HE ARRIVES AT THE HOTEL IN MARSEILLE.
WITH CHAIN HOTELS THERE'S NO SURPRISE...QUALITY, COMFORT, A BOTTLE OF WATER ON THE DESK, SATELLITE T.V., ALL-YOU-CAN-EAT BREAKFAST BUFFET...
A REAL CONSTANT.
4:00 PM. THE TRAIN STOPS.
AN ANIMAL ON THE TRACKS.

THE 50-MINUTE DELAY CAUSES HIM TO MISS HIS TRAIN FOR MARSEILLE. NOT TO WORRY, HE'LL CATCH THE NEXT ONE. THERE ARE SLOWDOWNS ON MÉTRO LINE 4. NO PROBLEM, HE'LL GET THE 13 TO SAINT-LAZARE AND SWITCH TO THE 14 AT GARE DE LYON.
IN THE MÉTRO HE CAN'T HELP STARING AT THE PRETTY - ALBEIT WEARY-LOOKING - WOMAN SITTING ACROSS FROM HIM. SHE GLANCES UP FROM HER FREE NEWSPAPER. HE SMILES AT HER.
SHE SMILES BACK, BEMUSED, AND GOES BACK TO HER NEWSPAPER. TOO BAD.
7:00 PM. ONCE SETTLED COMFORTABLY IN HIS SEAT ON THE HIGH-SPEED TRAIN FOR MARSEILLE, MARTIN CALLS LÉA FOR THE DAY'S NEWS. LEA STOPPED WORKING WHEN THEIR FOURTH CHILD WAS BORN.
CAN YOU IMAGINE? THEY WON'T EVEN DELIVER OUT HERE... 250 EUROS!
YEAH, WHAT A HASSLE. DO YOU WANT ME TO PICK IT UP ON MY WAY HOME TOMORROW?
NO, THAT'S ALL RIGHT. I'LL ASK DAD. OR ROLAND. HE HAS TO COME PICK UP THE LAWNMOWER ANYWAY.
PERFECT! IS HUGO ALREADY IN HIS ROOM? HE'S GOT SOMETHING TO RECITE TO ME.
NO, I'LL GET HIM FOR YOU.
YEAH, YEAH, I KNOW, DAD. CAT: C-A-T. MAP: M-A-P. HAVE: H-A-V.
UH, IS THAT ALL?
UH, H-A-V...
H-A-V-E. START AGAIN, HUGO...

11:29 PM. MARTIN ARRIVES AT SAINT-CHARLES STATION IN MARSEILLE. MARTIN ENJOYS THESE TRIPS, WHICH IS WHY HE LOVES HIS JOB SO MUCH. WITH HIS SENIORITY, HIS SALES FIGURES AND HIS PEOPLE SKILLS, HE'S BEEN OFFERED PLENTY OF PROMOTIONS. BUT HIS ANSWER IS ALWAYS THE SAME:
NO WAY! LOCK ME UP IN AN OFFICE AND I'LL QUIT!
IT'S BEEN A LONG DAY. MARTIN WON'T BE GOING TO BED LATE TONIGHT. HE STILL TAKES TIME TO ORGANIZE: TOMORROW'S CLOTHES ON THE CHAIR, TABLET PLUGGED IN AND SUITCASE NEXT TO THE WARDROBE.
IBIS STYLES HOTELS
IN BED, HE THINKS ABOUT NEXT SUMMER. IT'S HIS TURN TO PUT TOGETHER THE NEXT FAMILY REUNION...

GABY

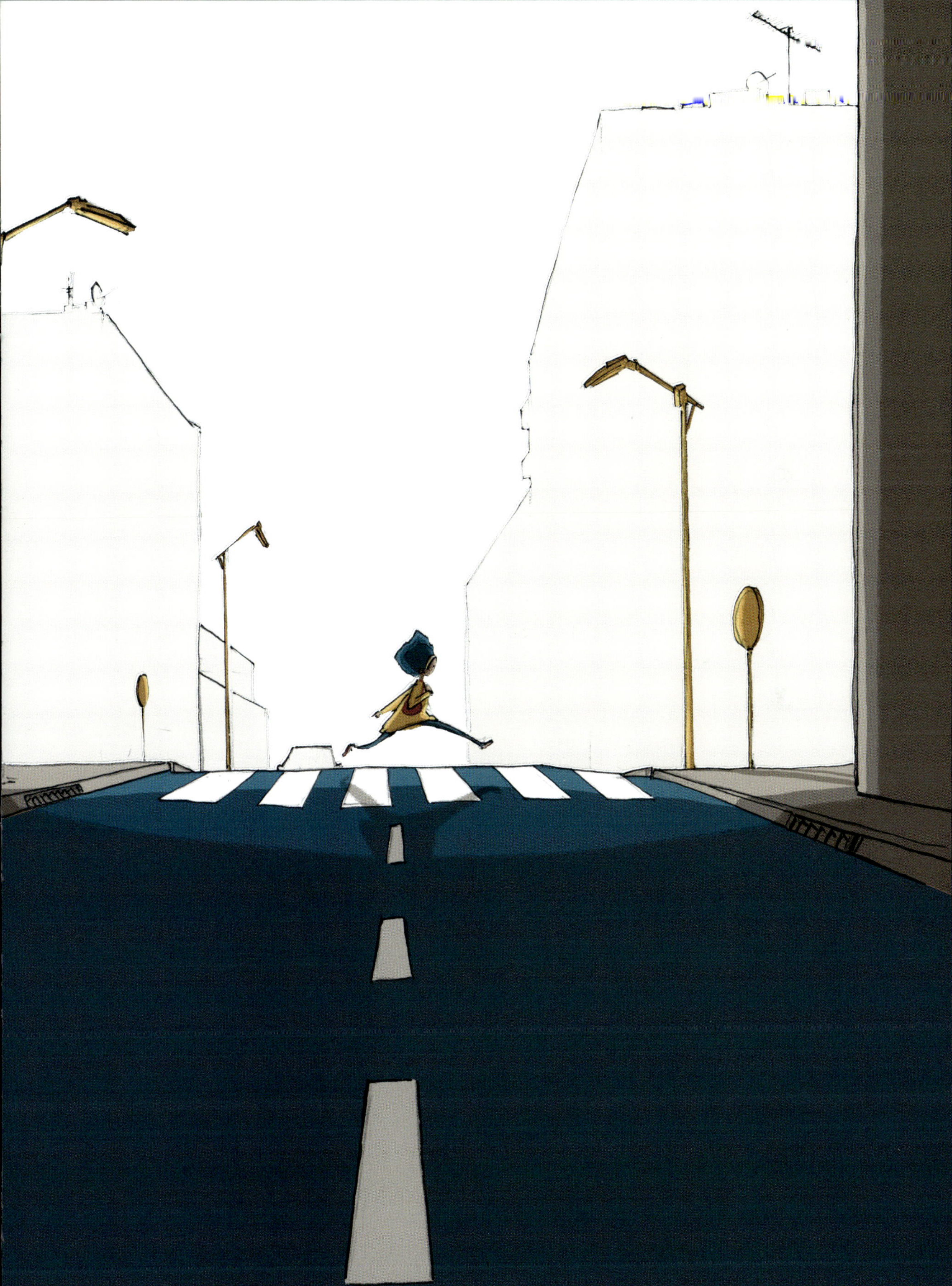

6:00 AM. THE ALARM GOES OFF IN GABY'S BEDROOM. SHE GETS UP RIGHT AWAY. IF SHE GAVE HERSELF EVEN THE SLIGHTEST BIT OF LEEWAY, SHE'D GO BACK TO SLEEP.
EVERY MORNING, GABY GIVES HERSELF TWENTY MINUTES OF TOTAL PEACE. TODAY SHE'S TIRED, AND PROMISES HERSELF THAT SHE'LL GET TO BED EARLY TONIGHT.
GABY'S LIFE IS HECTIC. SHE HAS TO DO EVERYTHING HERSELF - THE KIDS, THE FLAT, THE JOB, THE SHOPPING, CHANGING THE LIGHT BULBS.
IT'S 7:40 AM.
JOËL, DON'T LET ALAIN RUN INTO THE STREET.
HOLD ON MÉLINA, I'LL HELP YOU ZIP YOUR JACKET.
SHE TAKES MÉLINA TO DAYCARE, ALAIN TO NURSERY SCHOOL AND JOËL TO PRIMARY SCHOOL.
HOME
DAYCARE
SCHOOLS
10 MIN
4 MIN
12 MIN
2 MIN
THEN GABY HEADS FOR THE TRAIN STATION TO CATCH THE INTER-CITY TRANSIT. SHE GRABS A FREE NEWSPAPER ON THE PLATFORM. FIRST THE NEWS, THEN HER HOROSCOPE.
METRO
"TODAY YOU'LL MEET SOMEONE WHO COULD CHANGE YOUR LIFE".
PFFF...IF ONLY...

FOR A YEAR NOW SHE'S BEEN MAKING HER WAY TO THE HOSPITAL, WHERE SHE WORKS AS A NURSE'S AIDE.

IN ALL, IT TAKES HER AN HOUR AND TWENTY MINUTES TO GET THERE, INCLUDING THE STOPS AT THE DAYCARE AND SCHOOLS, THE BUS, THE TRAIN AND THE MÉTRO. ALL DURING RUSH HOUR, OF COURSE.

SOMETIMES, SHE FEELS A BIT LOST.

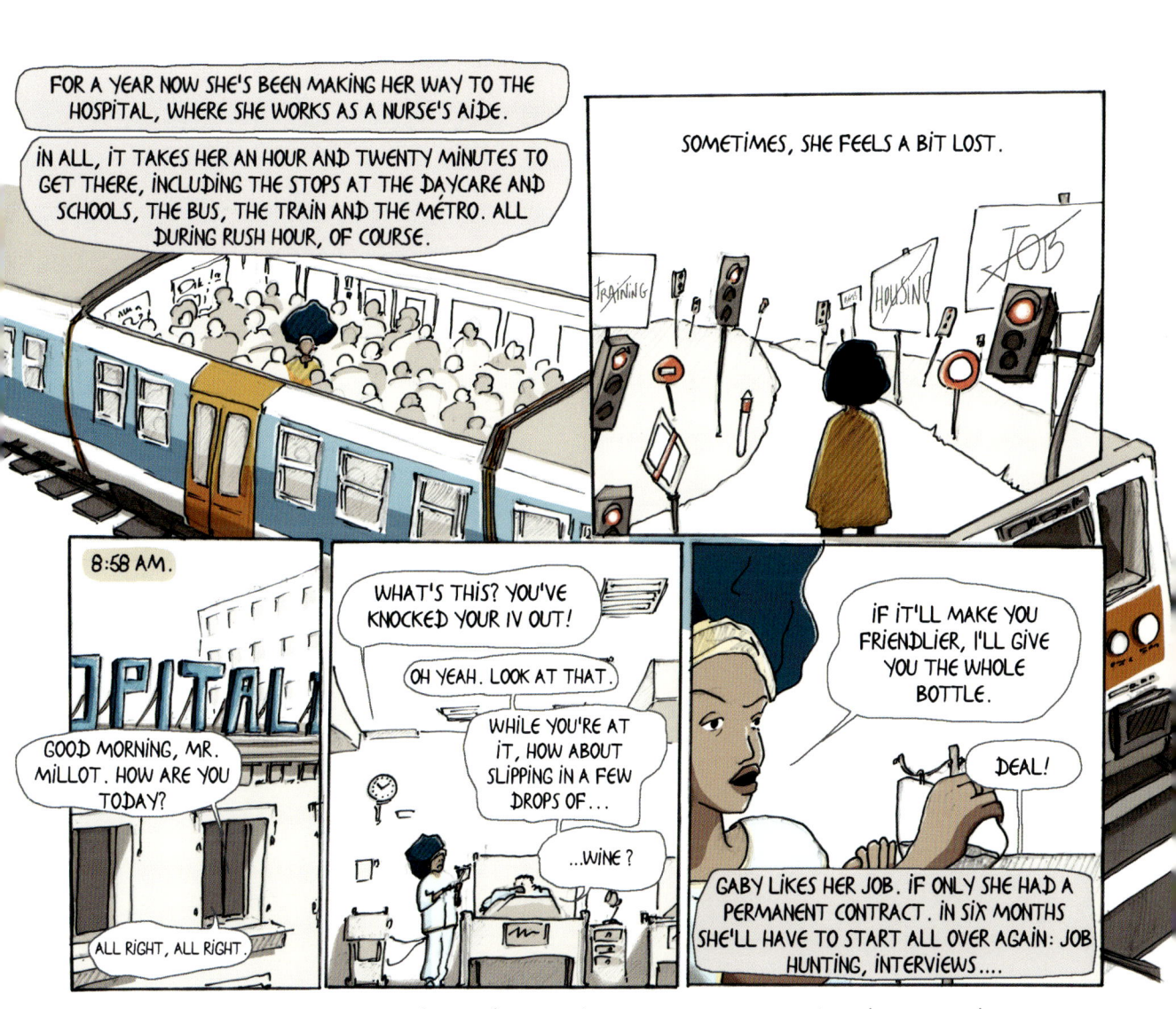

8:58 AM.

GOOD MORNING, MR. MILLOT. HOW ARE YOU TODAY?

ALL RIGHT, ALL RIGHT.

WHAT'S THIS? YOU'VE KNOCKED YOUR IV OUT!

OH YEAH. LOOK AT THAT.

WHILE YOU'RE AT IT, HOW ABOUT SLIPPING IN A FEW DROPS OF...

...WINE?

IF IT'LL MAKE YOU FRIENDLIER, I'LL GIVE YOU THE WHOLE BOTTLE.

DEAL!

GABY LIKES HER JOB. IF ONLY SHE HAD A PERMANENT CONTRACT. IN SIX MONTHS SHE'LL HAVE TO START ALL OVER AGAIN: JOB HUNTING, INTERVIEWS....

BUT TO GO WHERE? THAT'S THE QUESTION. WHILE THERE'S NO LACK OF JOBS AROUND PARIS, THE HOSPITALS ARE ALL FAR AWAY. AND GABY DOESN'T HAVE A DRIVING LICENSE.

SHE'S WILLING TO COMMUTE. AND ANYWAY, SHE HAS TO WORK. THERE'S RENT AND BILLS TO PAY, AND THERE'S MELINA, ALAIN AND JOËL...

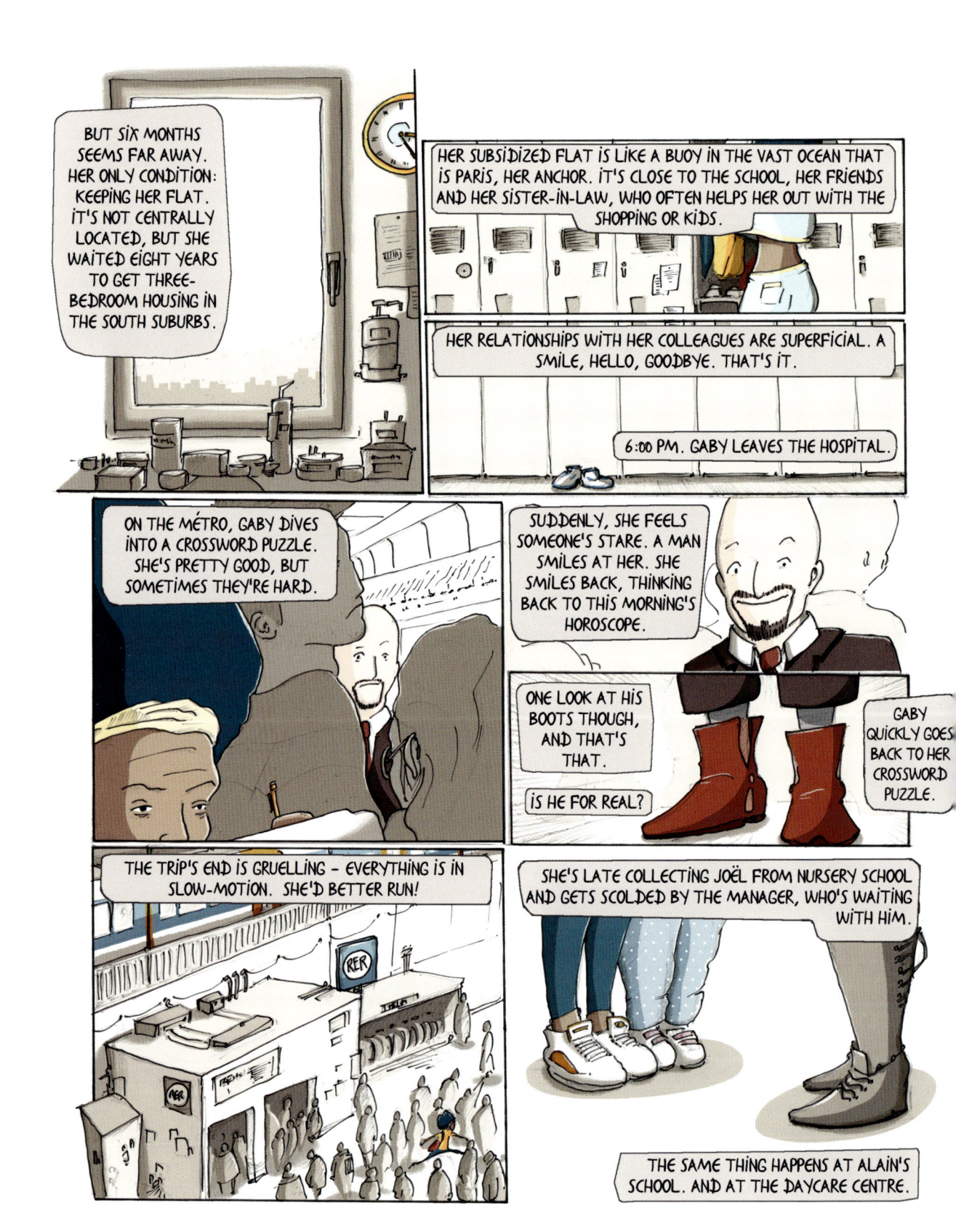

BUT SIX MONTHS SEEMS FAR AWAY. HER ONLY CONDITION: KEEPING HER FLAT. IT'S NOT CENTRALLY LOCATED, BUT SHE WAITED EIGHT YEARS TO GET THREE-BEDROOM HOUSING IN THE SOUTH SUBURBS.

HER SUBSIDIZED FLAT IS LIKE A BUOY IN THE VAST OCEAN THAT IS PARIS, HER ANCHOR. IT'S CLOSE TO THE SCHOOL, HER FRIENDS AND HER SISTER-IN-LAW, WHO OFTEN HELPS HER OUT WITH THE SHOPPING OR KIDS.

HER RELATIONSHIPS WITH HER COLLEAGUES ARE SUPERFICIAL. A SMILE, HELLO, GOODBYE. THAT'S IT.

6:00 PM. GABY LEAVES THE HOSPITAL.

ON THE MÉTRO, GABY DIVES INTO A CROSSWORD PUZZLE. SHE'S PRETTY GOOD, BUT SOMETIMES THEY'RE HARD.

SUDDENLY, SHE FEELS SOMEONE'S STARE. A MAN SMILES AT HER. SHE SMILES BACK, THINKING BACK TO THIS MORNING'S HOROSCOPE.

ONE LOOK AT HIS BOOTS THOUGH, AND THAT'S THAT.

IS HE FOR REAL?

GABY QUICKLY GOES BACK TO HER CROSSWORD PUZZLE.

THE TRIP'S END IS GRUELLING - EVERYTHING IS IN SLOW-MOTION. SHE'D BETTER RUN!

SHE'S LATE COLLECTING JOËL FROM NURSERY SCHOOL AND GETS SCOLDED BY THE MANAGER, WHO'S WAITING WITH HIM.

THE SAME THING HAPPENS AT ALAIN'S SCHOOL. AND AT THE DAYCARE CENTRE.

SHE ALSO COLLECTS JESSICA, HER NEIGHBOURS' DAUGHTER. THEY OFTEN HELP EACH OTHER OUT.

YET ANOTHER REASON WHY SHE LIKES WHERE SHE LIVES.

WITHOUT THESE HELPING HANDS, SHE'D HAVE A HARD TIME MAKING IT. DAILY LIFE IS A REAL OBSTACLE COURSE...

AS SHE RUSHES TO GET SUPPER READY, HER EYES SETTLE ON THE CRACK IN THE KITCHEN WALL. SHE'LL HAVE TO REMEMBER TO CALL THE PUBLIC HOUSING OFFICE...FOR THE THIRD TIME.

AFTER THE KIDS ARE IN BED, GABY COLLAPSES ON THE COUCH AND GRABS THE REMOTE. JUST THEN, THE DOORBELL RINGS.

IT'S NADIA, A NEIGHBOUR, WHO'S COME TO TALK ABOUT HER PROBLEMS. SOMETHING ABOUT INSURANCE. GABY LISTENS POLITELY WITHOUT REALLY FOLLOWING.

BY THE TIME NADIA LEAVES, GABY'S COMPLETELY EXHAUSTED. STILL, SHE GOES BETWEEN THE NEWS, A DOCUMENTARY ON WILD BEAST MIGRATION AND THE END OF A SERIES SHE HAS TROUBLE KEEPING UP WITH...FOR A GOOD HOUR.

11:10 PM. GABY FALLS ASLEEP IN FRONT OF THE T.V. WITH HER BACK KILLING HER. BETWEEN THE PUBLIC TRANSPORT AND WORK, SHE'S BEEN ON THE MOVE ALL DAY.

GETTING TO BED EARLY ? NICE TRY...

THIERRY

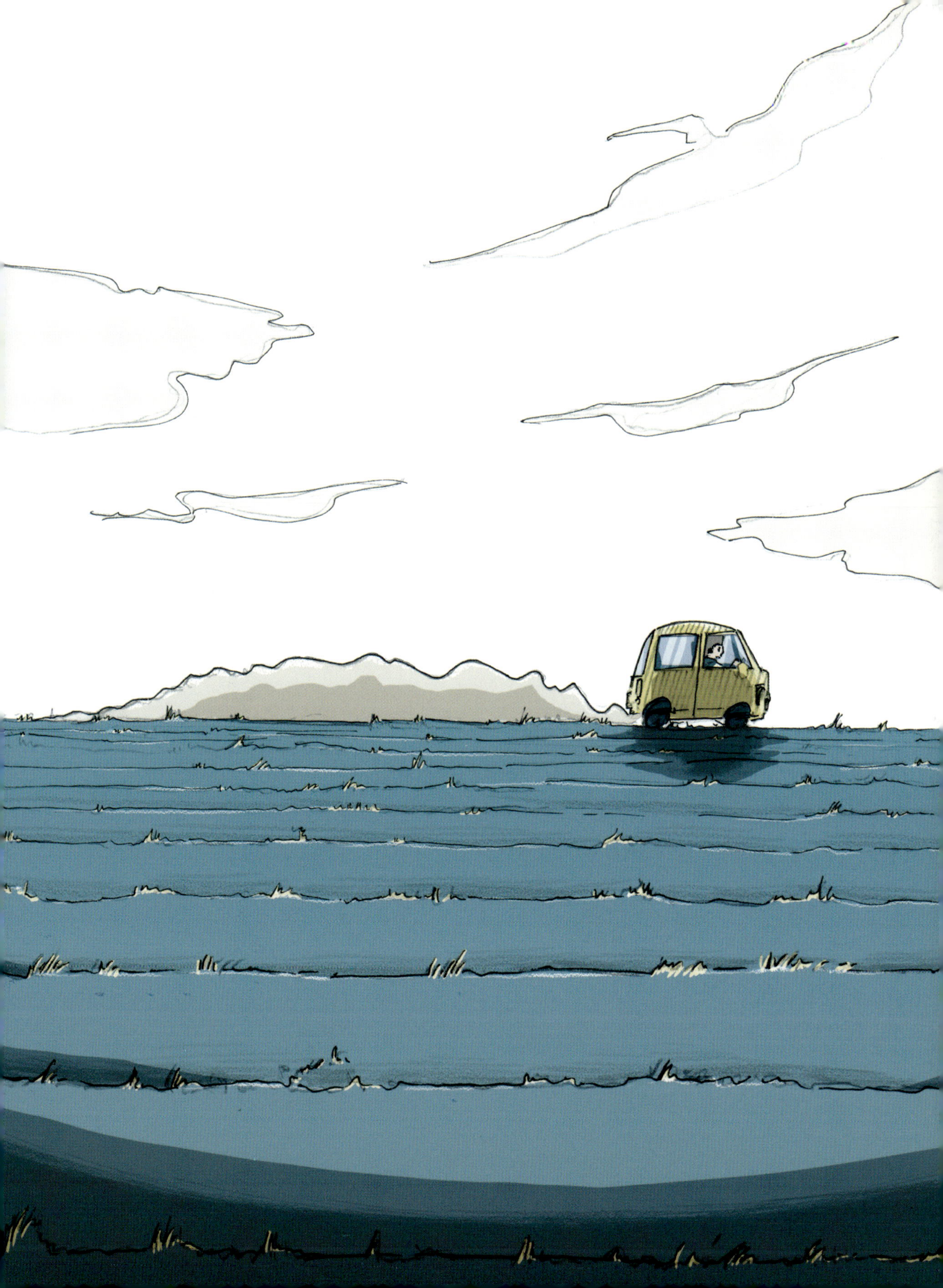

LAST NIGHT, CARQUEFOU BEAT DUNKERQUE ON THEIR HOME TURF. DENIS RENAUD'S PLAYERS TOOK THE UPPER-HAND IN THE 58TH MINUTE. 1 TO 0, THE TEAMMATES....
CLICK.
7:09
YESTERDAY FILIPPETTI ANNOUNCED PLANS TO REFORM THE STATUS FOR ARTISTS
CLACK.
7:19
MEOW ?
SHOWERS IN THE SOUTH-EASTERN PORTION OF THE COUNTRY. THE CLOUDS WILL GIVE WAY TO SUN IN THE LATE AFTERNOON. A SUNNY DAY IN BREST. UNUSUALLY COLD IN NICE TODAY.
BAM!
MEOW ?
THIERRY, NEARLY 40, IS A FLUTE TEACHER, AND SINGLE BY CHOICE, WELL...ALMOST SINGLE.
MEOW ?
HE'S LIVED WITH HIS NOW-BLIND CAT, GISCARD, FOR 20 YEARS.
DURING BREAKFAST HE THINKS ABOUT WHAT HIS DAY WILL BRING. WILL MAËLLE HAVE DONE HER EXERCISES? WILL ALBIN BE ABLE TO CONCENTRATE? WILL MARGOT'S CONCERT BE A SUCCESS?
MEOW ? MEOOWW ?
COMING, GISCARD!
THIERRY GIVES LESSONS AT THREE MUSIC SCHOOLS AND PRIVATELY AT STUDENTS' HOMES IN THE NANTES AREA.
BUT IT'S NOT ENOUGH TO MAKE ENDS MEET. SO HE ALSO DOES TUTORING AND SOME HANDIWORK FOR THE NEIGHBOURS.
HIS BUSY SCHEDULE TAKES HIM FROM ONE END OF THE REGION TO THE OTHER.
LUCKY HE'S GOT HIS CAR!

ON THE ROAD THE RADIO BROADCASTS A BARRAGE OF NEWS BRIEFS AND MORNING TALK SHOWS WITH TASTELESS JOKES...

HE SWITCHES STATIONS EVERY TIME HE SWITCHES GEARS, AN OLD HABIT.

8:15 AM. THE DRIVE IS MONOTONOUS. HE'S HAVING A HARD TIME CONCENTRATING. TOO BAD. HAD HE BEEN LISTENING, HE WOULD HAVE HEARD THAT FC NANTES IS PLAYING AT HOME TONIGHT.

HE'S DISTRACTED. AT THE RAILROAD CROSSING, WITHOUT SO MUCH AS EVEN GLANCING AT THE PASSING TRAIN FULL OF PEOPLE, HE WONDERS IF HE SHOULD GET PETROL BEFORE WORK.

DETOUR. WITH HALF A TANK HE SHOULD BE ABLE TO MAKE IT UNTIL FRIDAY OR SATURDAY. BUT THERE'S NO GUARANTEE...

8:30 A.M. THIERRY STOPS AT THE PETROL STATION. 25 EUROS IN THE TANK, LEAVING HIM 300 IN HIS ACCOUNT.

A FEW MINUTES LATER, HE ARRIVES AT SCHOOL FOR THE MORNING.

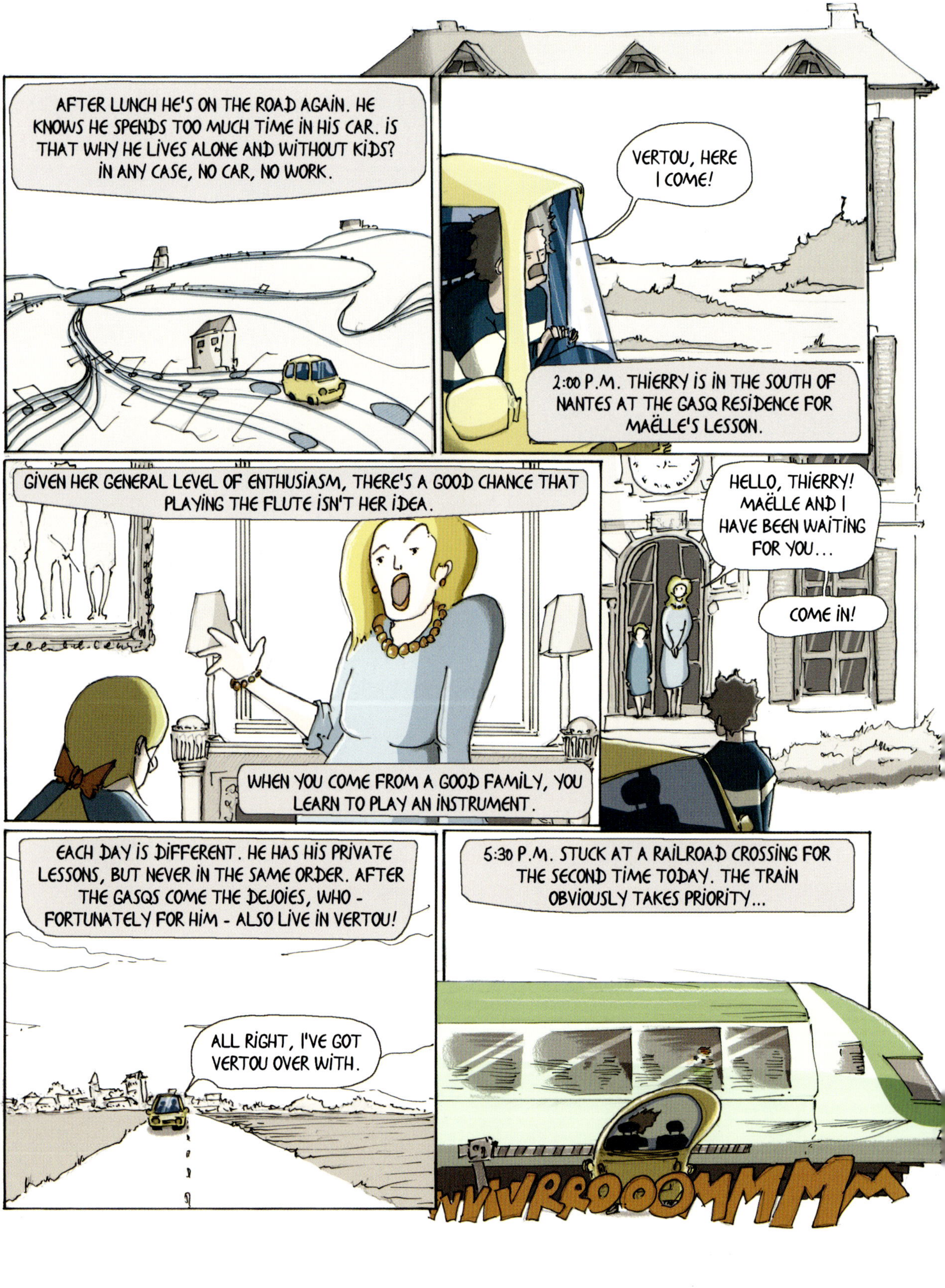
AFTER LUNCH HE'S ON THE ROAD AGAIN. HE KNOWS HE SPENDS TOO MUCH TIME IN HIS CAR. IS THAT WHY HE LIVES ALONE AND WITHOUT KIDS? IN ANY CASE, NO CAR, NO WORK.
VERTOU, HERE I COME!
2:00 P.M. THIERRY IS IN THE SOUTH OF NANTES AT THE GASQ RESIDENCE FOR MAËLLE'S LESSON.
GIVEN HER GENERAL LEVEL OF ENTHUSIASM, THERE'S A GOOD CHANCE THAT PLAYING THE FLUTE ISN'T HER IDEA.
WHEN YOU COME FROM A GOOD FAMILY, YOU LEARN TO PLAY AN INSTRUMENT.
HELLO, THIERRY! MAËLLE AND I HAVE BEEN WAITING FOR YOU...
COME IN!
EACH DAY IS DIFFERENT. HE HAS HIS PRIVATE LESSONS, BUT NEVER IN THE SAME ORDER. AFTER THE GASQS COME THE DEJOIES, WHO - FORTUNATELY FOR HIM - ALSO LIVE IN VERTOU!
ALL RIGHT, I'VE GOT VERTOU OVER WITH.
5:30 P.M. STUCK AT A RAILROAD CROSSING FOR THE SECOND TIME TODAY. THE TRAIN OBVIOUSLY TAKES PRIORITY...
VVVVRROOOMMMM

BACK HOME FOR A QUICK BREAK, JUST LONG ENOUGH TO FEED GISCARD.

Y'A DES CIGALES DANS LA FOURMILIÈRE ET VOUS N'POUVEZ RIEN Y FAIRE Y'A DES CIGALES DANS LA FOURMILIÈRE ET C'EST POUR ÇA QUE J'ESPÈRE...

THIERRY RENTS HIS PLACE. NO WAY HE COULD POSSIBLY GET A LOAN WITHOUT A STABLE JOB.

NO BIG DEAL! HE FEELS COMPLETELY AT HOME IN HIS "COCOON", AS IF IT WERE HIS OWN.

HIS FRIENDS LIVE IN THE NEIGHBOURHOOD. SO DO HIS BROTHER AND SISTER. AND THIERRY'S GOTTEN TO KNOW HIS NEIGHBOURS. HE OFTEN DOES THEM FAVOURS - SOMETIMES FOR A FEE.

TODAY IT'S MARCEL'S TOILET. 10 MINUTES OF WORK AND A 40-MINUTE MONOLOGUE ABOUT THE WORLD MOVING TOO FAST.

8:30 P.M. TIME FOR THE CONCERT. MARGOT HAS BEEN HIS STUDENT FOR SEVEN YEARS. POULENC'S SONATA. SHE GIVES SUCH A HEARTFELT RENDITION.

11:30 P.M. THIERRY'S TIRED. 50 MINUTES GETTING HOME FROM THE CONCERT. HIS BACK HURTS BECAUSE OF THAT BLASTED FOOTBALL GAME. NEARLY THREE HOURS IN THE CAR TODAY. OF COURSE, TOMORROW'S SCHEDULE WILL BE DIFFERENT.

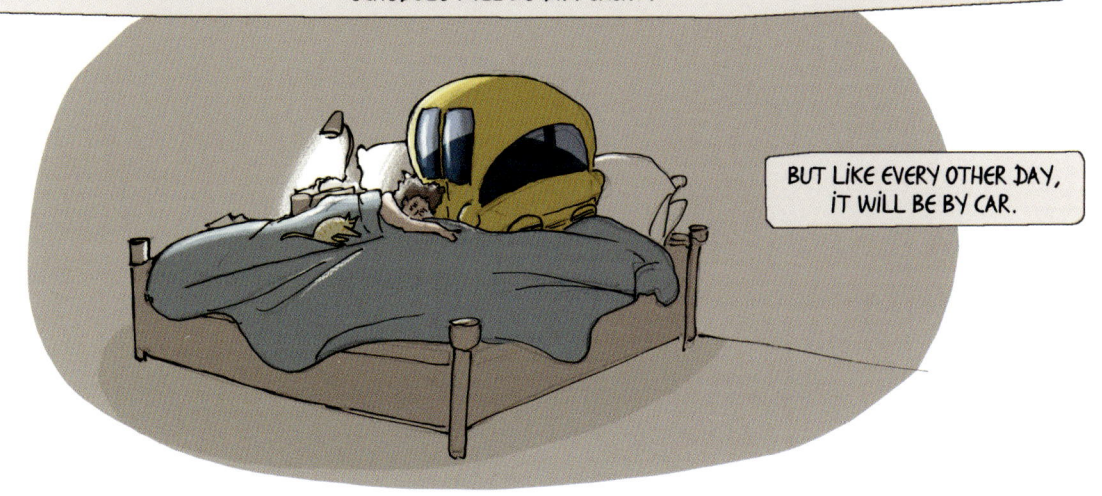

BUT LIKE EVERY OTHER DAY, IT WILL BE BY CAR.

CHRISTELLE

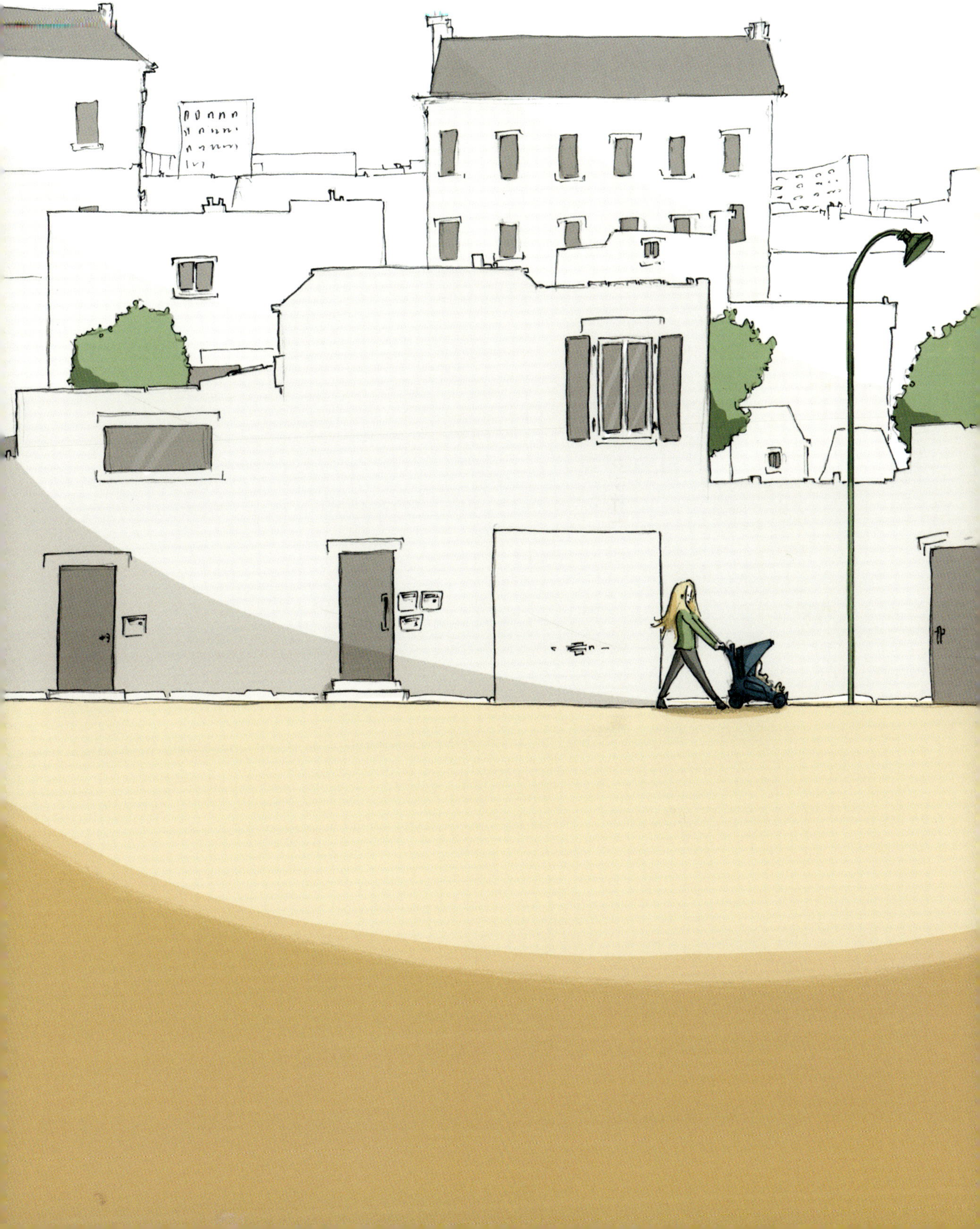

6:30 AM.

Aggrrrr...

Bonjanjou... doll!

ihiiih...

6:33 AM.

GOOD MORNING, ANTOINE. HOW CAN YOU BE SO QUIET WITH A NAPPY THAT SMELLS SO BAD?

LET'S GET YOU CHANGED.

CHRISTELLE RELISHES HAVING BREAKFAST AT HOME EVERY MORNING, NOT IN SOME HOTEL ON THE OTHER SIDE OF FRANCE. SHE DOESN'T REGRET FOR ONE SECOND HER DECISION TO CHANGE JOBS AND PUT AN END TO THE BUSINESS TRIPS HER PREVIOUS POSITION DEMANDED. IT JUST WASN'T COMPATIBLE WITH FAMILY LIFE.

YET, SHE LIKED THE TIME SHE SPENT ON THE ROAD, HER LITTLE BLACK SUITCASE AND, MOST OF ALL, THE FREEDOM OF MOBILE LIFE.

BUT WHAT'S THE POINT OF HAVING CHILDREN IF SOMEONE ELSE HAS TO RAISE THEM?

CHRISTELLE AND PATRICK DROP ANTOINE OFF AT THE DAY CARE CENTRE TOGETHER BEFORE HEADING TO THEIR RESPECTIVE JOBS.

7:46 | 7:49 | 7:52 | 7:55 | 7:57

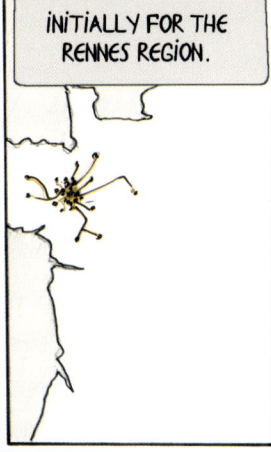

CHRISTELLE HANGS UP HER COAT AND PURSE AND TURNS ON HER COMPUTER. NOW SHE'S THE ONE IN CHARGE OF SETTING THE SALES TEAM'S OBJECTIVES...

WHICH SHE'S QUITE GOOD AT, HAVING WORKED AS A SALES REP HERSELF FOR SEVERAL YEARS...

INITIALLY FOR THE RENNES REGION.

THEN FOR THE WHOLE WEST OF FRANCE. ALWAYS WITH THE SAME INSURANCE COMPANY.

ON THE ROAD MONDAY THROUGH FRIDAY, A DIFFERENT HOTEL EVERY NIGHT, SUIT HANGING IN THE BACK OF THE CAR, AN EMERGENCY SET OF TOILETRIES ALWAYS READY IN THE CORNER OF HER SUITCASE.

SHE'S EVEN GOT A TRAVEL IRON. COMFORTABLE BEING BEHIND THE WHEEL - NO NEED FOR A GPS - CHRISTELLE DISCOVERED MANY CHARMING TOWNS AND RESTAURANTS DURING HER SALES TRIPS.

TWO YEARS AGO, WHEN SHE TOLD HER SUPERVISORS SHE WANTED A MORE SEDENTARY POSITION, SHE WASN'T EXPECTING THEM TO GIVE HER A PROMOTION.

WE'RE VERY HAPPY WITH YOUR WORK. WE'RE THINKING OF YOU FOR THE TEAM COORDINATOR POSITION. WHAT DO YOU THINK?

AT 36, AFTER 8 YEARS OF MARRIAGE, IT WAS TIME TO THINK ABOUT STARTING A FAMILY. AND PATRICK WAS GETTING IMPATIENT.

1:15 CHRISTELLE AND PATRICK OFTEN MEET FOR LUNCH. IT'S PRACTICAL WHEN YOU WORK IN THE SAME CITY.

YOU HAD THE STEAK YESTERDAY. WAS IT GOOD?

AS ALWAYS!

EGG-MAYONNAISE AND STEAK IT IS, THEN.

A COFFEE AND THE CHECK, PLEASE!

WHEN SHE GETS BACK TO THE OFFICE, CHRISTELLE MAKES SURE HER STAFF ARE ALL ON THE ROAD.

ONCE THAT'S DONE, SHE DIVES INTO THE FILES THAT HAVE BEEN PILING UP ON HER DESK SINCE THIS MORNING.

AT THE BUS STOP, CHRISTELLE HAS SIX MINUTES BEFORE THE BUS COMES. JUST ENOUGH TIME TO SMOKE A CIGARETTE, A BAD HABIT SHE'S RECENTLY PICKED UP AGAIN.

COULD IT BE THAT SHE'S A BIT BORED?

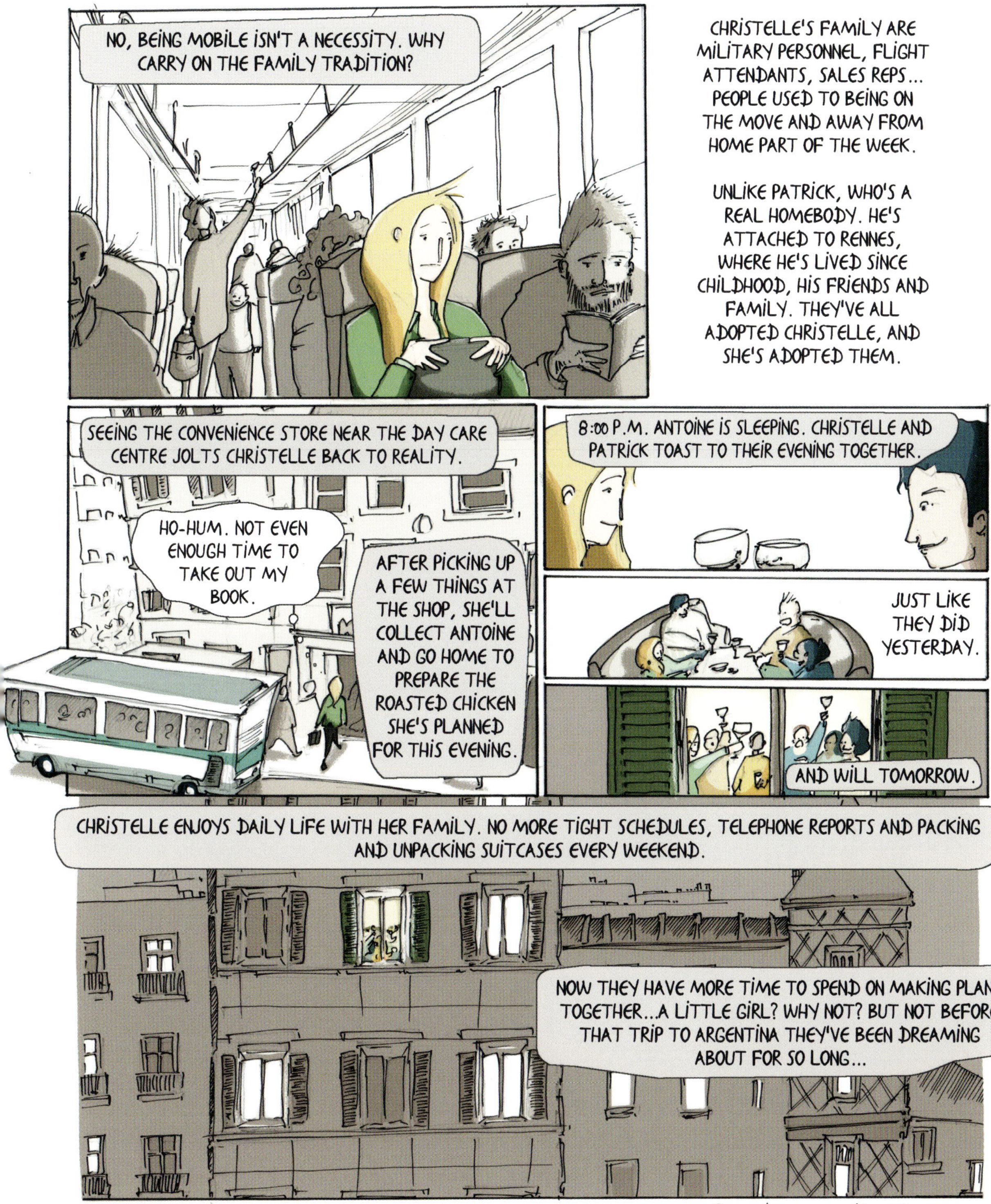

Jean Leveugle, Léa Mazé, 2014

BEHIND THE DRAWINGS

JEAN, EMILIE, MARTIN, GABY, THIERRY, CHRISTELLE…

…are not entirely fictional characters. You might even know them, especially given that they are representative of a significant portion of workers in our societies today.

These working people have one point in common: they spend (or spent) a lot of time traveling for work. Regardless of the distance they travel, this time spent traveling – often far from home - structures their personal experience, giving rise to a very specific lifestyle known as "high mobility".

The study of work-related high mobility shows a new relationship to space and time, a relationship that that goes beyond the mere question of transport offering by shedding light on the complex choices people must make at different times in their lives to balance the demands of work and personal life.

THE TRYPTICH OF WORK-RELATED HIGH MOBILITY

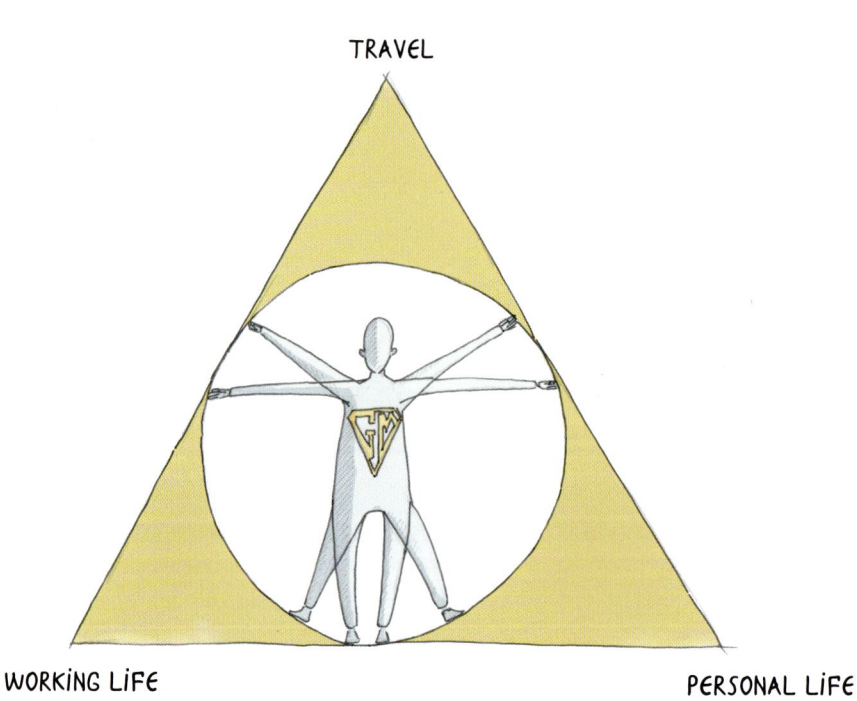

TRAVEL

WORKING LIFE　　　　　　　　　　　PERSONAL LIFE

Is it possible to raise our children when we spend more nights sleeping in hotels than at home? Can we continue living in our native region without risking unemployment? Are a passport and suitcase essential for a career? Should we spend hours commuting each day to stay in the home we've renovated? Does finding a job mean accepting a highly mobile lifestyle? And so forth. All of these questions and a number of others inspired a group of researchers to conduct a sociological survey of highly mobile professionals in Germany, Spain, France and Switzerland.

The six cartoon portraits have offer a glimpse of what mobile life is. Here are a few more keys for a deeper understanding this phenomenon.

THE RESEARCH PROJECT

THE RESEARCH ON WHICH THE PORTRAITS AND RESULTS PRESENTED IN THIS BOOK ARE BASED AIMS TO BETTER UNDERSTAND THE WORK-RELATED HIGH MOBILITY PHENOMENON AND ITS IMPACT ON PEOPLE'S WORKING AND PERSONAL LIVES.

THE EUROPEAN RESEARCH PROJECT BEGAN IN 2006 IN SIX COUNTRIES - GERMANY, BELGIUM, SPAIN, FRANCE, POLAND AND SWITZERLAND - AS PART OF THE "JOB MOBILITIES AND FAMILY LIVES" PROGRAMME.

THE FIRST WAVE OF THE STUDY, BASED ON A STATISTICAL SURVEY OF 7220 PEOPLE, WAS COMPLETED IN 2010.

IN 2011 AND 2012, A SECOND WAVE WAS LAUNCHED IN FOUR OF THE SIX COUNTRIES - GERMANY, SPAIN, FRANCE AND SWITZERLAND - AMONG 1985 RESPONDENTS. THOSE SURVEYED IN 2007 WERE RE-INTERVIEWED. IN ADDITION, 40 INDIVIDUALISED INTERVIEWS OF HIGHLY MOBILE OR FORMERLY-HIGHLY MOBILE INDIVIDUALS WERE CONDUCTED AS WELL.

10 TEAMS WERE INVOLVED IN THE PROJECT OVER SIX YEARS (SEE PAGE 81).

IDENTIFYING HIGHLY MOBILE INDIVIDUALS

Through the portraits, our first goal was to emphasise the extremely ordinary nature of high mobility. We are surrounded by people who either spend a great deal of time commuting to work each day, or who spend the working week away from their partners because their workplaces are geographically far apart, or who travel the region, the country and the world as part of their job.

ONE OUT OF TWO PEOPLE PRACTICES WORK-RELATED HIGH MOBILITY AT ONE POINT OR ANOTHER IN THEIR CAREER

In 2007, between 18 and 25% of European households were affected by high mobility. Among adults aged 25 to 54, 9% were highly mobile and 8 to 11% had a mobile partner. In addition to those identified as highly mobile at the time of the interview, it appears that high mobility is a phase that many experience at one time or another. In 2011, many of the 30 to 59 year-old respondents had experienced a period of high mobility (from 38% in Spain to 57% in France).

As the graphs (right) show, high mobility decreased slightly between 2007 and 2011 among respondents, confirming the hypothesis that such phases are less frequent as people get older.

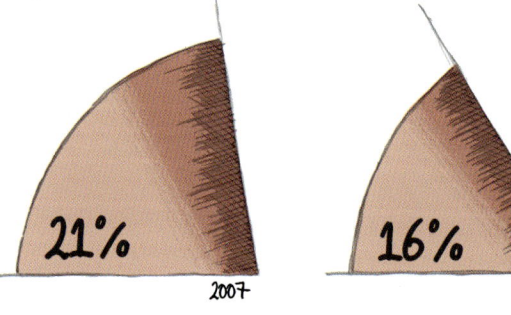

21% 2007

16% 2011

PERCENTAGE OF HOUSEHOLDS AFFECTED BY HIGH MOBILITY
(SPAIN, FRANCE, SWITZERLAND AND GERMANY)

Our image of highly mobile people as scurrying hurriedly between flights or trains in dark suits, a briefcase in one hand and a suitcase on wheels trailing behind, is a kind of caricature (among our "characters", Martin undoubtedly comes the closest). In fact, high mobility includes a wide range of situations and practices that reflect as many different ways of living - as the five other portraits illustrate. Balancing a job – fulfilling, if possible – and a rich, happy personal and social life is the main goal of most highly mobile people. However, it is often a challenge, especially for working couples, as the home and workplace are often geographically distant.

So, who are these highly mobile people? If a suit and briefcase don't define them, what does?

Gender and household structure are useful elements to consider when it comes to distinguishing highly mobile people. In 2011, 13% of men aged 30 and 59 were highly mobile, versus 7% of women (note that this difference was not due to a higher working rate among men). Regarding household structure, single-parent families stood out with twice as many highly mobile individuals as those with partners and children (15% versus 8%).

People like Gaby, a single mother, must single-handedly cope with the time and spatial constraints of domestic, family and working life. The need for steady income adds to time and organizational constraints, especially as regards children. Our research furthermore shows that such individuals also tend to have erratic mobility practices, and start and stop high mobility situations more than other people.

Beyond gender and household structure, our research found that income is not necessarily a determinant of high mobility. In other words, contrary to popular belief, high mobility is practiced among both the affluent (Martin, Christelle, Emilie and Jean) and the less well-off (Gaby and Thierry). Similarly, education has little impact on high mobility practices. Regarding age, we found that highly mobile workers were not necessarily among the youngest. The social and demographic variability of highly mobile people led us to look more closely at why people become highly mobile and the way they experience high mobility.

TWICE AS MANY MEN AS WOMEN ARE HIGHLY MOBILE

DAILY MOBILITY

The research indicates that the many high mobility forms and practices must be considered in connection with balancing personal and professional life.

Family ideals and career goals are sometimes difficult to reconcile, given geographical constraints. Commuting, sometimes even long distances, is one way of resolving this issue. This is why we try to show the personal and professional situations and conditions of travel (transport mode(s), use of travel time, positive or negative perception of travel time, etc.) for each of the six character portraits.

Yet, these portraits go even further by attempting to bring to life a set of research results regarding people's relationship to high mobility.

RESIDENTIAL LOCATION: LITTLE IMPACT ON HIGH MOBILITY PRACTICES

One of our most important findings concerns access. Regardless of the quality of the transport access, the impact on high mobility practices was marginal, except as concerns long-distance daily commuting (or commuter trips), which was more common in 2007 among respondents living in highly urbanised areas with better access. In 2011, however, highly mobile respondents were as likely to live in urban areas as peri-urban and rural ones – i.e. areas with good access vs. those with inferior access. The portraits also show the variety of residential contexts of highly mobile people: dense urban centres (Christelle and Thierry), small cities (Emilie), peri-urban areas (Gaby and Jean) and rural areas (Martin).

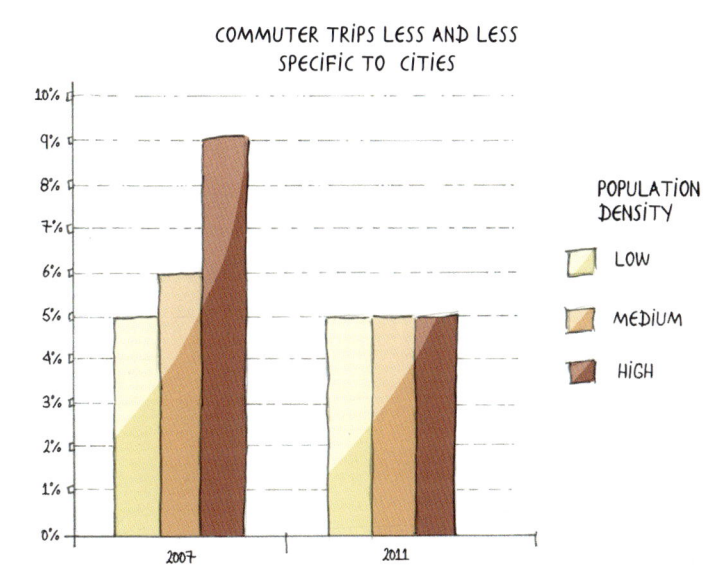

COMMUTER TRIPS LESS AND LESS SPECIFIC TO CITIES

POPULATION DENSITY
- LOW
- MEDIUM
- HIGH

HIGH MOBILITY AND COUPLE/FAMILY RELATIONSHIPS: A DELICATE BALANCE

Jean's profile highlights another important characteristic of high mobility, namely the weakening of marital ties, particularly when one of the partners overnights regularly. Hence, between the two survey waves (2007 and 2011), 13% of mobile male respondents living with a partner had separated, whereas this figure was only 9% for non-mobiles. Among mobile female respondents, 17% no longer lived with their partner, versus 8% for non-mobiles.

TOMORROW NICOLE IS GETTING UP EARLY TO GO TO THE GYM WITH BRIGITTE AND LAURENCE. FOR ONCE, JEAN WILL BE THE ONE DRIVING THE GIRLS TO SCHOOL. FEELING A BIT LOST, HE GOES UP TO BED. SOMETIMES, HE WONDERS JUST WHERE "HOME" REALLY IS.

More detailed statistical analyses helped determine that the weakening of marital ties due to high mobility mainly affected women without children and men with children.

> AT 36, AFTER 8 YEARS OF MARRIAGE, IT WAS TIME TO THINK ABOUT STARTING A FAMILY. AND PATRICK WAS GETTING IMPATIENT.

Among women, motherhood often coincided with a rejection of high mobility, whereas fatherhood changed nothing from this standpoint. Christelle's profile reflects this: she willingly chose to give up her frequent business trips to start a family, proving that family life and parenthood are seen as incompatible with high mobility.

51% of men who were mobile in 2007 were no longer so in 2011 if they had not had a child, versus 59% who had had one. Among women, 56% continued to be mobile if they had not had a child. 83% no longer were if they had. And when it was their first child, high mobility stopped altogether!

THE BIRTH OF A CHILD HAS A STRONGER IMPACT ON WOMEN

83% OF WOMEN STOP BEING HIGHLY MOBILE AFTER HAVING A CHILD

59% OF MEN STOP BEING HIGHLY MOBILE AFTER HAVING A CHILD

One thing, however, is clear: high mobility delays the arrival of children, or at least a first child, for both men and women. Yet, differences between the sexes do exist here. For one, in families with several children, high mobility is easier for the man than for the woman. Not surprisingly, the partners of mobile people often find jobs close to home, or even give up their own careers. This is what we attempted to show with Martin's character. His mobility is made possible by his wife's immobility, whose daily life if quite local.

As we can see, all high mobility depends on immobility, be it at home or at work. We also noted that high mobility reinforced traditional gender roles when there were children present, with women acting as guardians of the hearth in their mobile partner's absence. The opposite, i.e. highly mobile mothers, is unusual, even though high mobility in such cases favours a more equal division of domestic tasks.

HIGH MOBILITY: A SHORT-TERM OR LONG-TERM SITUATION?

Our survey data shows that high mobility may be considered either in the long term - as an inherent part of the career path - or as a phase. We distinguished four character types based on how mobility plays a part in their life stories (see graphs pages 54-55).

The first type reflects early and short mobility. These individuals enter the labour market relatively early and have a single, short period of high mobility between ages 20 and 25.

54

FROM FIRST JOB TO RETIREMENT, FOUR TYPICAL HIGH MOBILITY PATHS

A SHORT MOBILITY EPISODE EARLY IN THE CAREER

PROGRESSIVE MOBILITY THROUGHOUT THE CAREER

How to read the graphs:
The working people questioned were divided into four distinct groups,
which describe four typical work-related high mobility paths.
For example, the first graph reads: of all the highly mobile people with short mobility
episodes early in their careers, 20% had a highly mobile job at age 20.

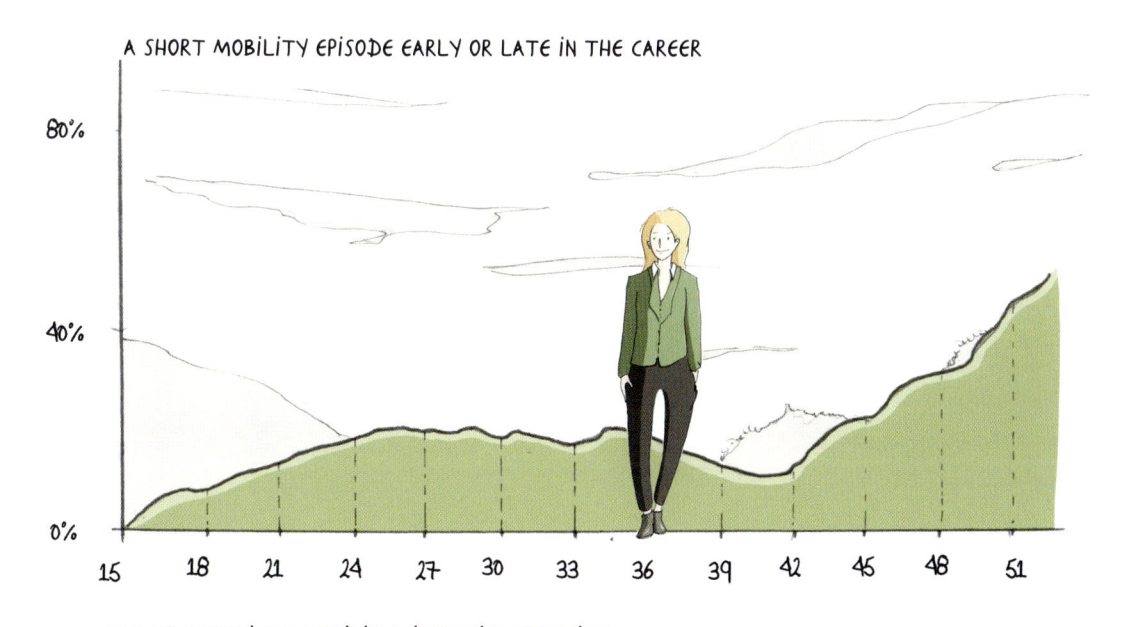

A SHORT MOBILITY EPISODE EARLY OR LATE IN THE CAREER

EARLY ENTRY INTO MOBILITY, INTENSIVE PRACTICE

This was the case for Emilie. For her, high mobility is merely a temporary situation that is unlikely to recur, due to the long commutes that create tension between her home and working life.

The second type also reflects early career mobility. However, these individuals – both younger and with a higher level of education – tend to enter the labour market later. While their period of mobility is typically temporary, some take it up again in their 40s (once their children are independent). Christelle is representative of this type group.

The third type reflects ongoing and temporary long-term mobility. Despite having very different lives, Martin and Thierry are both representative of this group.

The fourth and final group includes people with ongoing daily mobility, like Gaby or Jean.

HIGH MOBILITY: A NORM?

Jean's mobility reflects that of many people with inherently mobile occupations.

Train driver as well as lorry driver, flight attendant, captain, sailor, military personnel and fire fighter are all occupations that inherently involve regular absences from home. These occupations are not new, and it is difficult to predict an eventual increase in the number of people employed in these sectors. For instance, the number of sales representatives of all types and ranks has steadily grown since the early 1980s, whereas the number of military personnel, police agents and fire fighters has fallen (job survey, INSEE). Beyond the fact that changes will undoubtedly occur, it is difficult to predict whether or not high mobility will increase in these occupations due to lack of data.

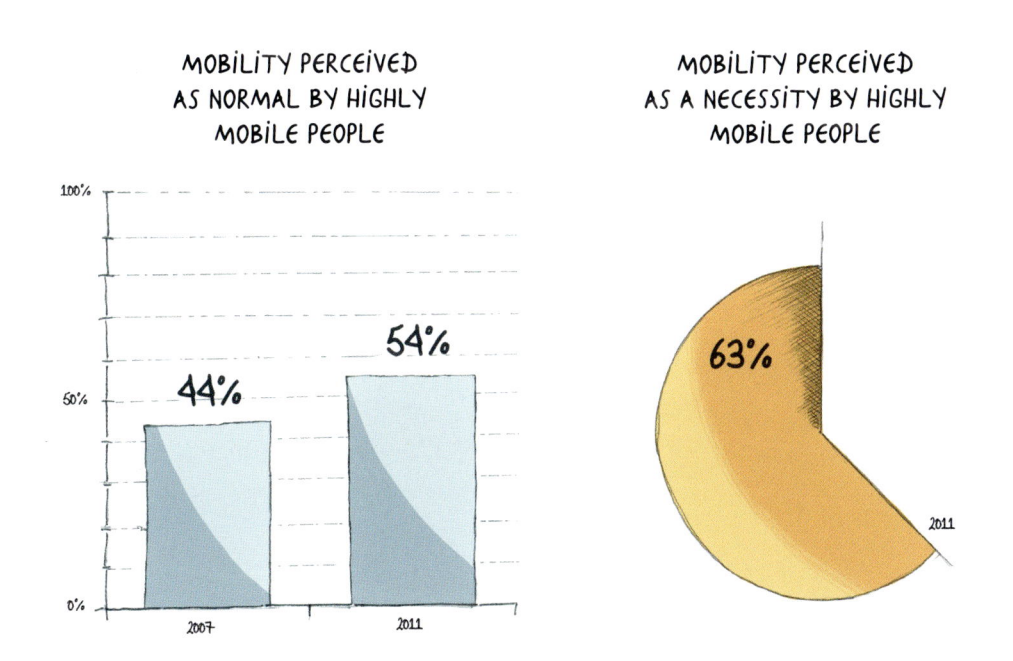

MOBILITY PERCEIVED AS NORMAL BY HIGHLY MOBILE PEOPLE

- 2007: 44%
- 2011: 54%

MOBILITY PERCEIVED AS A NECESSITY BY HIGHLY MOBILE PEOPLE

- 2011: 63%

Jean sees the fact that he spends a lot of time travelling as neither negative nor positive. For him, it is simply a fact of life, an inherent part of his chosen occupation. In this respect, he is very much representative of a large percentage of highly mobile people. In France, Germany, Spain and Switzerland in 2007, 44% considered high mobility as "normal". In 2011-2012, this figure rose to 54%. 63% even saw high mobility as a necessity. In addition to those for whom high mobility was an integral part of their job, high mobility was viewed as "normal" among a growing number of individuals.

THE IMPACT OF ECONOMIC CONDITIONS ON HIGH MOBILITY

If high mobility seems increasingly to be becoming necessary — even normal — for balancing personal and professional life, it is largely due to the major economic downturn in the recent years. With increasing unemployment, high mobility is imposed on those with the least job security. 45% of respondents in 2011 confirmed this fact.

It is for this reason that Thierry is forced to make frequent, sometimes distant commutes. His piecemeal jobs and high mobility reflect an unstable situation that changes in nature and intensity from job to job. High mobility can also be protection against unemployment. It allowed 62% of the highly mobile respondents aged 30 to 59 surveyed in 2011 to get out of unemployment or avoid it. In Spain this figure was nearly 80%.

However, not everyone is equal when it comes to high mobility. While access to transport is difficult for Gaby, it is not an issue for Christelle. Organizational and time management skills, the ability to get about in unfamiliar places and being comfortable interacting with strangers are also essential for high mobility. Such skills can be acquired early on and thus become a form of inequality. While Martin and Christelle are well prepared in this sense, Thierry and Emile are not.

DIFFERENT APTITUDES FOR MOBILITY

Our six mobile narratives show that, while high mobility is becoming a norm, individuals' skills nonetheless differ greatly. Our study was based on the concept of motility, that is, each person's mobility 'potential'. This potential is composed of: (1) the transport offering, (2) personal mobility skills and plans and (3) the desire to be mobile. In our survey, we considered that rapid transport access (highways, high-speed trains, airports, etc.), personal skills in terms of mobility (knowing how to read a map, find one's way, speak several languages, etc.) and people's disposition to mobility (willingness to move, to commute more than two hours a day, to make frequent business trips, etc.). Based on these criteria, six groups emerged.

The first two include those with weak mobility skills and those, on the contrary, with strong ones. Thierry and Martin perfectly illustrate this contrast (see graph page 62).

Those in Thierry's group have weak motility and are also proportionally the largest group. While their access to transport systems is average, their personal resources in terms of mobility are weaker, due notably to their poor linguistic skills and unwillingness to be mobile. Many of the people in this group were adults under 60. As people get older, their mobility potential may decrease due to physical disability, difficulty adapting to and making use of new technology, and/or the desire for greater stability and hence less willingness to make major changes. However, this may not necessarily be the case for younger generations when they reach age 50.

The second group includes people with strong motility, good access to transport systems and excellent skills. People in this group — primarily young men — are willing to be mobile regardless of the form of mobility. Often childless, though sometimes with partners, these individuals usually have few family constraints to consider when seizing employment opportunities, regardless of the location and form(s) of mobility required. Few are homeowners, which is consistent with their weak attachment to their residential location, and many have lived abroad. Martin is a good example. He is very comfortable in transport and travelling to new places, and has no apprehension about his upcoming trip to China. He knows how to manage time and space, and is able to anticipate and improvise — useful skills when travelling.

The other groups in our typology are hybrids of these two extremes. The third and fourth groups include people whose plans are at odds with their skills and access. In other words, what they want to do and what they can do are not consistent. Christelle and Gaby are two examples of this.

People in the third group — of which Christelle is a member — are characterised by their unwillingness to be mobile despite good access, skills and salaries, showing that even those best equipped may refuse high mobility. Their position on mobility tends to be long-term; rarely were they mobile in the past (unlike Christelle). Many, however, had migrated, undoubtedly to avoid long commutes or overnighting. All of this underscores the desire for a sedentary lifestyle and strong attachment to a home. As in the unmotile group, women outnumbered men here.

In contrast, the fourth group — which includes Gaby — is characterised by limited skills, average access and a strong disposition to mobility. Its members are forced to be mobile due to difficult economic and social circumstances. Their weak language skills and the fact that few had ever moved more than 70 miles for work-related reasons does not stop them from declaring themselves willing to migrate or travel frequently. Men, single people and those with only average training are likely to be in this group. In most cases, they were not homeowners, perhaps in part due to an inability to settle down in one place.

The last two groups help illustrate the trade-off of moving versus commuting. Emilie daily commutes to avoid moving — which she does not want to do — making her a member of the fifth group. People in this group have good transport access and skills, but prefer reversible mobilities such as long-distance

> BUT TO GO WHERE? THAT'S THE QUESTION. WHILE THERE'S NO LACK OF JOBS AROUND PARIS, THE HOSPITALS ARE ALL FAR AWAY. AND GABY DOESN'T HAVE A DRIVING LICENSE.
>
> SHE'S WILLING TO COMMUTE. AND ANYWAY, SHE HAS TO WORK. THERE'S RENT AND BILLS TO PAY, AND THERE'S MELINA, ALAIN AND JOËL...

commuting and overnighting (having a secondary residence near the work place). The composition of this group is quite diverse, with no clear tendencies in terms of age, gender or education level. We were able to determine, however, that its members often live with their families, have high incomes and are attached to their city or town.

The sixth and final group does not appear in our portraits. Emilie does, however, encounter one of its members. These individuals are characterised by excellent access, skills and their willingness to migrate inter-regionally or internationally, or make frequent business trips. We noted that such people were unlikely to long-distance daily commute or overnight (i.e. regular reversible mobilities), and tended to be young men with good educations and incomes.

> BY THE WAY, DID YOU ASK FOR YOUR TRANSFER?
>
> YEAH, BUT IT'LL TAKE A GOOD FIVE YEARS.
>
> I DON'T KNOW HOW YOU DO IT. I MOVED CLOSER TO THE SCHOOL AFTER SIX MONTHS.

This willingness to move is closely linked to weak place attachment (to a home, city or country). The predominance of renters among non-reversibles confirms this tendency.

A MOBILE COMMUNITY
PERCENTAGE SHARE FOR EACH GROUP

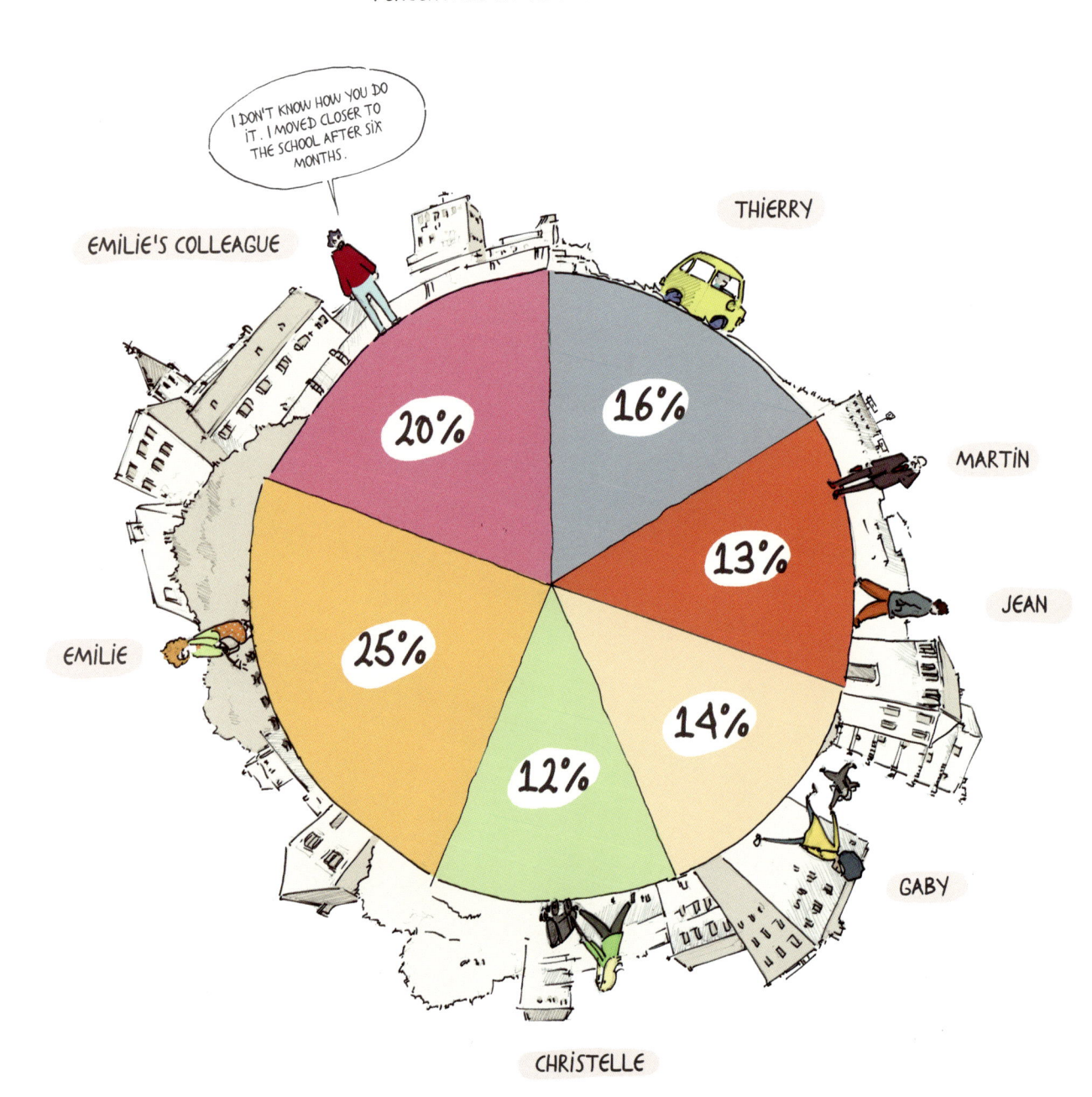

EMILIE'S COLLEAGUE: *I don't know how you do it. I moved closer to the school after six months.*

- THIERRY: 16%
- MARTIN: 13%
- JEAN: 14%
- GABY: (unlabeled)
- CHRISTELLE: 12%
- EMILIE: 25%
- (pink segment): 20%

A VARIETY OF EXPERIENCES

Our observation of the impact of financial circumstances and differences in people's willingness to become highly mobile has led to an important finding: namely, that high mobility is experienced differently by different people.

Christelle's case aptly illustrates this: those who experience high mobility the most positively and find it most rewarding are also those with the greatest capacity to put an end to it. People like Gaby and Thierry, for whom mobility is problematic, have no real way of avoiding it. A wide range of factors explain these differences, from lifestyle to marital status, the notion of 'quality of life', parenthood, mobility skills, economic conditions, and even social position. Our research shows that whether or not high mobility is experienced positively or negatively is closely linked to personal attributes, both individual and interpersonal. Thus, it is not merely a question of providing high-quality transport service. While comfort and ergonomics undoubtedly facilitate the use of travel time, they do not automatically make mobile people happy with their mobile lives. Emilie maximises her travel time by working or relaxing thanks to her modal choices, which enable her to experience a situation, she neither desires nor hopes will be long-term, more positively.

Like Emilie, Martin knows how to optimise his travel time by working. Just as he is able to work outside of the office, he also knows how to be at home without actually 'being there'. His long-term high mobility and the pleasure he takes in it are largely due to his ability to manage places, time and activities in a disconnected way, thus creating permeability between the work and family spheres.

> FOR A YEAR NOW SHE'S BEEN MAKING HER WAY TO THE HOSPITAL, WHERE SHE WORKS AS A NURSE'S AIDE.
>
> IN ALL, IT TAKES HER AN HOUR AND TWENTY MINUTES TO GET THERE, INCLUDING THE STOPS AT THE DAYCARE AND SCHOOLS, THE BUS, THE TRAIN AND THE MÉTRO. ALL DURING RUSH HOUR, OF COURSE.

For Gaby, however, her travel time is merely wasted time due to difficult physical conditions (peak hours and difficulty getting a seat). Hence, high mobility is a tedious situation to which she has resigned herself, given that she has no other choice from a financial standpoint.

CHANGES IN HOW HIGHLY MOBILE PEOPLE MAKE USE OF THEIR TRAVEL TIME

+13% PER YEAR — FREQUENT OVERNIGHTERS, LIKE MARTIN, SPEND MORE AND MORE OF THEIR TRAVEL TIME ON **LEISURE ACTIVITIES**

+8% PER YEAR — COMMUTERS LIKE EMILIE SPEND MORE AND MORE OF THEIR TRAVEL TIME **RELAXING**

+7% PER YEAR — HIGHLY MOBILE PEOPLE LIKE MARTIN AND EMILIE USE MORE AND MORE OF THEIR TRAVEL TIME FOR **WORKING**

HIGH MOBILITY: A SOCIAL INDICATOR

All of these portraits — and through them all of our research findings — show how going beyond the notion of transport and travel as mere flows and mechanical fluidity is necessary for understanding high mobility. Being mobile is not simply going from point A to point B, like random particles in a flow of passengers in a Métro car. We must look at the particles that *compose* the fluid, because each of these particles has a personal (and professional) history, skills and plans. Similarly, each trip takes on deeper meaning based on the context, time frame, constraints and location in (and under) which it occurs and whether or not it is work-related. Of course, we are talking about people, not particles. Similarly, we must no longer talk about transport but mobility.

This sociological effort has led us to put greater emphasis on the extremely diverse potentials of different persons. Access to transport, mobility skills and plans, together form the basis for people's mobility potential. These three elements, however, are not generic determinants, and greatly depend on context; while mobility skills are fuelled by mobility experiences all through life, transport offers are specific to their territories. Moreover, territories have varying degrees of potential receptiveness depending on the nature of people's plans and specific high mobility needs in terms of services, transport infrastructure and spatial organization.

High mobility offers a rich, comprehensive lens through which to better understand territories, work and families, but above all, the way in which people — with their personal histories, skills and dispositions — combine these elements in their daily lives.

What will the future bring? Will Gaby and Thierry continue being highly mobile out of economic necessity? Will Emilie succeed in putting an end to her long commutes? Contrary to the popular belief that high mobility is a growing trend in contemporary societies, our research results — based on a temporal approach to high mobility — prompt us to be somewhat cautious. High mobility practices are not more prevalent among younger generations than among older ones. However, the complexity of mobile paths and the instability with regard to situations of high mobility seem to be increasing. Although people are increasingly faced with high mobility, the episodes are relatively short, though much more frequent. In this respect, high mobility is but another sign of the growing uncertainty in contemporary societies (both at home, due to the weakening of marital ties, and in the workplace, due to economic dynamics). It is undoubtedly no coincidence that people who spend a lot of time commuting are not more likely to live in big cities than in peri-urban or rural areas.

While these underlying trends strongly influence high mobility, they leave room for government authorities and transport operators to manoeuvre. Beyond the development of ever-more diverse, high-performance transport offerings, the future of high mobility in our societies will also depend on changes in household structures, the fluidity of the housing market, changes in labour laws and numerous other non-transport-related factors, including women's role in the labour market and the division of gender roles within the family. Impacting high mobility must occur not only through transport policy, but within the larger framework of developing a veritable policy as regards mobility.

For the complete research report on highly mobile people, visit:
http://fr.forumviesmobiles.org/projet/jobmob

POLITICAL DESIGNS

BY SYLVIE LANDRIÈVE, CHRISTOPHE GAY AND MARC PEARCE

High Mobility: A Societal Phenomenon

In the past several decades, the distance between the home and workplace has continued to grow. With increases in transport speeds, one can work a hundred miles from home without having to relocate. We immediately think of this lifestyle of so-called "reversible" mobility as being the prerogative of business people, corporate executives, researchers and high-powered lawyers, like George Clooney's character in *In the Air*. Yet, we forget that those most concerned by high mobility are long-distance transport drivers. What has changed, however, is that many other service sectors - including sales, teaching and administration - are now affected as well. In fact, today, half of working households in France include a highly mobile person at one time or another.

Whether the job involves a two-hour daily commute, making frequent business trips or "overnighting", high mobility has become a societal phenomenon. In fact, we could say that this lifestyle that obliges so many to travel for work, while attempting to stay locally 'rooted', is emblematic of modern life. But what do highly mobile people really think?

A European research project helped us define them at the social level, to find out what they think, feel and want, and to better understand their practices, experiences and desires — in other words, to understand their way of life. In keeping with this research conducted in Germany, Spain, France and Switzerland in 2007 and again in 2011, the Mobile Lives Forum aims to propose tools for developing and implementing veritable *mobility* policies, not just transport policies. Its goal is to reach all those affected by work-related mobility. This includes collective entities such as businesses and government administrations with highly mobile employees, decision makers and services responsible for economic development, transport, family and gender equality. However, it also includes individuals who, mobile or not, will also find interest in the Forum's research and findings.

HIGH MOBILITY: A CHALLENGING CAREER PHASE

The European survey shows that people increasingly consider becoming highly mobile at some point in their careers — sometimes even at several different points, but for short periods. Nowadays it is difficult to categorically avoid or refuse this way of life. In general, however, people tend not to do it for long, except in the case of mobile occupations (pilot, chauffeur, driver or delivery person) or business reps, whose mobility is likewise part and parcel of their business. People become highly mobile essentially for practical reasons, i.e. in the hopes of getting a promotion or during hard times that call for a lifestyle change (unemployment, separation, etc.), often resigning themselves to it, more out of necessity than for pleasure. This clearly challenges the image of mobility as freedom.

Increasingly, highly mobile people describe their lifestyle as exhausting, arduous, trying and unenriching (except perhaps financially). Whether they know it or not, they are jeopardising the cohesion of their family unit, as well as that of their network of friends, and impeding their involvement in local life.

Research has already pinpointed certain effects of highly mobile lifestyles on health (fatigue), family (risk of separation) and social life (less socializing), which makes studying its other potential effects all the more interesting (the social cost of education at a distance, children's schooling, stress, etc.). There is a pressing need to increase social awareness about highly mobile lifestyles - not only among employers and politicians but also among workers themselves, and perhaps in society as a whole. In order to reduce this arduousness, we must imagine how to accompany the phenomenon, facilitate the lives of highly mobile people and perhaps even promote the development of less trying, more sustainable alternative lifestyles.

Identifying and assisting highly mobile people

This was our main finding from analysing highly mobile people's perception of their lifestyles.

Our results stress the importance for companies with highly mobile employees to revisit their human resource policies. While we are well aware of the existence of inherently mobile occupations, i.e. lorry drivers, train drivers, pilots, etc., new mobile occupations must also be identified.

Developing the skills necessary for high mobility

A policy that aims for employee well-being must first identify the positions that involve high mobility and assign them to those best suited for them, namely those without children or with adult-aged children. The European study also shows that jobseekers, often desperate to find a job at any cost, are more willing to be highly mobile than other people. In Spain, many job seekers and unstably employed people have become highly mobile since the 2008 economic crisis. In France, where the economic situation is more favourable, the phenomenon tends to affect single parents, those with weak skills and other such groups. Nonetheless, if the economic situation continues to worsen, high mobility could potentially increase. Political guidance would be useful in this case, especially given that the research has shown that a significant portion of the population does not know how to utilise its skills, i.e. how to use local transport or develop a plan to work abroad, to become highly mobile.

Companies could develop special travel training programs (reading maps, spatial orientation, using communication technologies, handling unforeseen events, cross-cultural socialising, etc.) for highly mobile employees and those organizing their trips. They could also provide information on the risks associated with high mobility for the individual and for the family. Prevention measures including regular check-ups to identify warning signs (changes in working hours, risk of burnout, changes in household structure) could also be implemented. Additionally, companies could do more to reward these newly-acquired skills and the practice of high mobility itself (especially travel abroad), particularly given that research has found that long-term high mobility, contrary to popular belief, does not increase the likelihood of having a higher income or getting a promotion.

FACILITATING HIGHLY MOBILE PEOPLE'S LINK WITH THEIR HOME PORT

The arduous nature of inherently mobile occupations has long been acknowledged in the form of ad hoc regulations, comp time, bonuses, etc. — measures that could also serve as a model for compensating high mobility. Companies today offer essentially material compensation, such as financial remuneration (for sales executives) or better comfort levels for travel (business class or first class on planes and trains) and accommodations (hotel chains). However, in order for the experience to be a positive one, highly mobile individuals must be able to rely upon strong support from family and friends. Contrary to the myth that a life of constant movement without bounds or ties is a good life, it would seem that the more mobile we are, the more stability we need. Perhaps that is a reason why the divorce rate is considerably higher among highly mobile people.

Based on this observation, companies could strive to facilitate contact between highly mobile employees and their 'home ports', by providing communication tools such as tablets with Skype or Facetime. This would allow them not only to see their families, but even to help their children with their homework. Facilitating high mobility also means helping the families of highly mobile people to better understand high mobility, and its advantages and disadvantages. Family members could occasionally be invited to accompany the highly mobile person on business trips.

Highly mobile people and their families could create exchange networks and discussion groups. Children could talk about their experiences so as to not feel isolated or alienated. Teachers could also learn more about this lifestyle and its impact on children (for instance, the impact of not having a daily relationship with a parent). Finally, two of our findings were linked to gender: first, couples wherein the female partner was mobile were less resilient than those wherein the male partner was mobile; second, the birth of a first child put a clear stop to women's mobility. These findings merit the implementation of mobility policies that take such findings into greater consideration.

REASSESSING THE FINANCIAL VALUE OF HIGHLY MOBILE PEOPLE'S TRAVEL TIME

Between 2007 and 2011 — the four years between the two survey waves — the percentage of highly mobile people who used their travel time for working increased by 30%. This was due to a number of factors, including growing tension in the labour market, thus resulting in an increase in the time spent working outside of the office. Add to this improved vehicle comfort and new technologies (tablets, smartphones, etc.), which can turn any place with a seat into a mobile office.

If such travel practices continue — or increase, as we hypothesise — public transport companies would do well to try and gain the upper hand vis-à-vis private cars. Companies would gain a real competitive edge by offering passengers veritable connected work spaces with Wi-Fi access, outlets for recharging devices (already available on certain trains), printing services and the possibility of purchasing computer accessories (adapters, chargers, etc.).

However, such changes also mean rethinking the economic value of travel time. Why not consider it as working time in its own right? Were this the case, we could be sure that companies would encourage their employees to use those modes of transport with the best working conditions. Transport operators could jointly develop ways of enhancing these modes turned into moving offices.

Decision makers would also be wise to improve comfort in existing modes of transport (increasing connectivity, reducing peak hours by staggering business office hours, etc.), rather than creating more infrastructure. Studies have shown that highly mobile people actually become relatively desensitized to the quality of access. Transport companies could therefore strive to make life better for mobile people by focusing on improving service speed and frequency and personally apprising travellers of traffic delays.

Mobility service companies could offer personalised training to mobile workers or human resource departments according to the type of mobility, whether high or not. They could target mobility organization by better managing the choice of itineraries and/or modes of transport used, the ability to use alternate routes, the use of travel time (by physically accompanying people on their first trip, etc.) and by improving how travel time is perceived (through stress management during delays).

REGULATING HIGH MOBILITY AND FACILITATING OTHER LIFESTYLES

High mobility is often seen as a step in the career path. From this standpoint, should we see the fact that it is less developed in France than in Germany and Switzerland as a form of resistance to modern lifestyles? Might it not be linked to the socio-economic structures of these countries, where women work less to facilitate the high mobility of their partners or spouses, and have fewer children? Possible future research topics... Today, however, we must start by recognising those who wish to limit their periods of mobility and by regulating work-related travel.

LIMITING THE NUMBER OF HIGHLY MOBILE POSITIONS

As highly mobile people tend to consider their situations temporary, companies could make an effort to limit the duration of their periods of high mobility, and even go so far as to reduce the number of highly mobile positions. Long-distance transport positions could also be revisited to limit overnighting.

EXPLORING OTHER MOBILITY SYSTEMS

Some of the systems that make it possible to work remotely — at home, in new co-working spaces or elsewhere — designed in the 1970s could now be developed thanks to the spread of new information technologies. In a more distant future, we could even imagine reducing the number and frequency of physical trips by creating position exchange networks. While this would give rise to its share of complications, especially as regards establishing a system of equivalence (i.e. remuneration or other benefits), it is worth testing, particularly for large businesses. The State could help in exploring the conditions under which such exchanges would be possible and create regulations to facilitate such practices.

Given the fact that our societies are likely to consume less energy in the future, such systems could result in more jobs closer to home — equally effective as the government-funded urban planning projects launched during the post war economic boom. Local production and short distribution channels could likewise contribute, as could new technologies like 3D printing.

The gap between research, managerial discourse, which often lauds people's ability to be mobile (i.e. their motility), and individuals' aspirations should lead to reforms not only in human resource policies but in mobility policies in general. For example, these policies shouldn't continue to ignore the importance of social and family relationships.

As we have seen, analysing the aspirations and perceptions of highly mobile people helps us question a contemporary social organisation founded on ever-increasing travel in a world confronted with issues of global warming and the depletion of energy resources. We could even posit that studying highly mobile people could help us define what "good mobile lives" will look like in the future, how to get there and what transition policies to adopt.

ABOUT THE AUTHORS

Emmanuel RAVALET has engineering training, as well as a PhD in transport economics from the University of Lyon and a PhD in urban studies from the INRS-UCS (Montreal). He currently works as a senior researcher at the Laboratory of Urban Sociology (LaSUR) at the École Polytechnique Fédérale de Lausanne.

Stéphanie VINCENT-GESLIN is research director at the Laboratoire d'économie des transports (LET) at the École nationale des travaux publics de l'État (ENTPE, Vaulx-en-Velin) and a research associate at the LaSUR (Lausanne). With a PhD in sociology from the University Paris-Descartes, her research focuses on understanding mobility behaviours and changes therein.

Vincent KAUFMANN is a professor of urban sociology and mobility analysis at the École Polytechnique Fédérale de Lausanne. He heads the laboratory of urban sociology (LaSUR) and is president of the steering and perspectives committee of the Mobile Lives Forum, the centre for research and exchanges created by SNCF for exploring future mobilities.

Jean LEVEUGLE is an urban planner and illustrator with a post-graduate degree in development (University of Paris 1 Panthéon-Sorbonne) and a graduate of the ENS of Paris and the Estienne School. Originally trained in sociology and political science, he works on questions of mobility, poverty and exclusion, and attempts to share and popularise the results of social science research through illustration.

Sylvie LANDRIÈVE is co-director of the Mobile Lives Forum. She is interested in the evaluation of public policies, particularly in regards to the organization of territories (urban planning, housing, transport). This is the common thread between her theoretical studies in the humanities (Sorbonne and Sciences-Po Paris), her management research (Mines, Nanterre and ESCP) and her work as a project coordinator for real estate and urban projects in the public and private sector (BNP Real Estate, SNCF).

Christophe GAY is co-director of the Mobile Lives Forum. His thinking is guided by questions of imaginaries, representations and social norms as determinants of lifestyles, especially those related to mobility now and in the future. This is why he proposed that SNCF, where he was formerly director of strategic communication planning, create the Forum. His areas of study include international law, political science and psycho-sociology (Sceaux, Sorbonne and Nanterre).

Marc PEARCE is in charge of piloting research projects and publishing their results for the Mobile Lives Forum. With degrees in sociology (Sorbonne) and urban planning (City University of New York, Institut d'Urbanisme de Paris and ENSA Paris-Malaquais), he is interested in forwarding knowledge dissemination methods and tackling critical issues associated with the visualisation of scientific data.

ACKNOWLEDGEMENTS

The researches would like to give special thanks to their "home ports": Mélanie, Zélie, Margot and Anouck; David and Albin; Anne, Valentin and Étienne.

The Mobile Lives Forum would like to thank the rail workers who helped better develop Jean's portrait, and Jean-Michel Ladoire and Philippe Gabriele in particular.

Jean Leveugle would like to thank Marie Gloor, Léa Mazé, Camille Crumeyrolle, Pierre Nocerino, Samuel Thomas and Martin Wacquez for their precious advice.

THE RESEARCH PROJECT

This book was made possible by the various research teams that participated in this project.

The LaSUR team in charge of the projects since 2011:

Stéphanie Vincent-Geslin
Emmanuel Ravalet
Vincent Kaufmann
Gil Viry
Yann Dubois
Maude Reitz

The teams involved since 2006:

- Johannes Gutenberg University of Mainz (Germany)
- Facultés universitaires Saint-Louis, Bruxelles (Belgium)
- Centre national de la recherche scientifique (France)
- Bundeswehr University, Munich (Germany)
- University of Warsaw (Poland)
- Universidad Autónoma de Madrid (Spain)
- École polytechnique fédérale de Lausanne - Laboratoire de sociologie urbaine (Suisse)
- Université de Genève (Switzerland)
- University of Applied Sciences, Nuremberg (Germany)
- Bundesinstitut für Bevölkerungsforschung (BiB), Wiesbaden (Germany)

The first survey wave (2006-2010) was funded by the 6th European Union program-framework.
The French and Swiss portions of the second wave (2011-2013) was funded by the Mobile Lives Forum.

ABOUT THE MOBILE LIVES FORUM

CREATED IN 2011, THE MOBILE LIVES FORUM IS AN INDEPENDENT INSTITUTE FOR RESEARCH AND EXCHANGE ON MOBILITY, SUPPORTED BY SNCF. UNDER THE SCIENTIFIC DIRECTION OF SOCIOLOGIST VINCENT KAUFMANN, IT STUDIES MOBILITY BOTH AS PHYSICAL MOVEMENT AND AS SOCIAL CHANGE. ITS GOAL IS TO PROVIDE MEANS FOR UNDERSTANDING, PREPARING FOR AND IMPACTING CHANGES IN MOBILE LIFESTYLES.

THE MOBILE LIVES FORUM IS PREPARING FOR THE MOBILITY TRANSITION. CONTEMPORARY WAYS OF LIFE ARE A SOURCE OF FREEDOM BUT OF FATIGUE AND ALIENATION AS WELL. CLIMATE CHANGES, THE DEPLETION AND RISING COSTS OF OIL, URBAN CONGESTION AND POLLUTION ARE IMPACTING AND WILL INCREASINGLY IMPACT THE BALANCE BETWEEN PHYSICAL TRAVEL, TELECOMMUNICATIONS AND OUR ACTIVITIES.

THE MOBILE LIVES FORUM IS DEDICATED TO RE-THINKING THIS BALANCE AND IDENTIFYING WHAT GOOD MOBILE LIVES COULD BE IN THE FUTURE, BOTH FOR INDIVIDUALS AND FOR SOCIETIES. IT ALSO AIMS TO IDENTIFY LEVERS FOR SPURRING CHANGE AT THE INDIVIDUAL, BUSINESS AND GOVERNMENT LEVELS.

A MULTI-DISCIPLINARY INSTITUTE, THE FORUM BRINGS TOGETHER RESEARCHERS FROM THE SOCIAL SCIENCES AND THE HUMANITIES, ARTISTS AND TRANSPORT AND URBAN PLANNING PROFESSIONALS. ITS APPROACH IS FOUNDED ON COMBINING EXPERIENCE, REASON AND EMOTION, IN ORDER TO WEAVE A NEW THREAD OF KNOWLEDGE AND UNDERSTANDING. AS A TRANSNATIONAL AND FREE-THINKING INSTITUTE, THE MOBILE LIVES FORUM LAUNCHES AND PROMOTES DEBATES, SUPERVISES RESEARCH, ORGANIZES EXPERIMENTS AND SHARES ITS FINDINGS INTERNATIONALLY, WITH A SPECIAL FOCUS ON CONTROVERSIES AND PIONEERING PERSPECTIVES THROUGH CONFERENCES, BOOKS AND ITS WEBSITE, AMONG OTHER THINGS.

THE FORUM IS HEADED BY ITS PRESIDENT, BERNARD EMSELLEM AND ITS CO-DIRECTORS CHRISTOPHE GAY AND SYLVIE LANDRIÈVE, WHO OVERSEE THE STEERING AND COORDINATION OF THE INSTITUTE'S ACTIVITIES.

To find out more and keep up on mobility, visit:
www.forumviesmobiles.org

Other Mobile Lives Forum publications:
MOBILE IMMOBILE (Paris, éditions de l'Aube, 2011)
REHABILITING THE PERI-URBAN (Paris, éditions Loco, 2013)
POST PETROLEUM (Paris, éditions Loco, 2014)

PRINTED IN JANUARY 2015
BY PERUZZO INDUSTRIE GRAFICHE, ITALY